HENRY H. PETERSOHN is a consultant in office automation, data communication, data processing equipment, and financial planning.

# Developing Computer Solutions For Your Business Problems

HENRY PETERSOHN

A SPECTRUM BOOK
Prentice-Hall, Inc./Englewood Cliffs, N.J. 07632

Library of Congress Cataloging in Publication Data

Petersohn, Henry H.
Developing computer solutions for your business problems.

A Spectrum Book
Includes index.
1. Business--Data processing. I. Title.
HF5548.2.P478 1982 658'.054 82-10188

ISBN 0-13-204313-0

ISBN 0-13-204305-X {PBK.}

This book is available at a special discount when ordered in large quantities. Contact Prentice-Hall, Inc., General Publishing Division, Special Sales, Englewood Cliffs, N.J. 07632.



A SPECTRUM BOOK



Printed in the United States of America

10 9 8 7 6 5 4 3

Prentice-Hall International, Inc., London
Prentice-Hall of Australia Pty. Limited, Sydney
Prentice-Hall of Canada, Inc., Toronto
Prentice-Hall of India Private Limited, New Delhi
Prentice-Hall of Japan, Inc., Tokyo
Prentice-Hall of Southeast Asia Pte. Ltd., Singapore
Whitehall Books Limited, Wellington, New Zealand

A special thanks to my wife Rosalind
for reviewing the drafts and making
editorial changes.

# Contents

# Preface

Managers and business executives in large organizations, as well as smaller companies, ask about using a computer to solve problems. It is not always practical to buy or lease a computer, and it is not necessary to know how to program to use a computer effectively. Although the manager or executive is responsible for the computer application, the detail work may properly be delegated to the data processing people. As a consultant, I have been asked: How do you get the data processing (DP) experts to understand what is wanted? How can you be sure that the DP experts will give you what is needed? How can you get them to change directions if your needs change? What choices are there in terms of cost versus service?

This book has been written to answer these questions, and to simplify the task of applying computer power to business problems. It guides you, the reader, in defining the problems, tells you how to explain your needs to the DP people, and points out how you can get the application installed as quickly and inexpensively as possible.

The text is organized into eight chapters, each covering a different aspect of a proposed application. The first chapter describes establishing application objectives and definitions; the second chapter focuses on alternative solutions which can be time and dollar savers. The third chapter describes how functional requirements are established, so that the DP people know what is intended. General implementation alternatives and installation are then discussed. The next two chapters describe how and where a management audit is desirable, and how to deal with privacy, security and backup requirements. The concluding chapter outlines trends in automation that can affect your computer application plans. Numerous illustrations and examples take you through the steps involved in successfully automating your application.

Henry H. Petersohn
Potomac, Md.

# Developing Computer Solutions For Your Business Problems

# 1

# Establishing application objectives and definition

## A. INTRODUCTION

A simple data processing application may involve a few pieces of existing equipment and several users at a single location. More complex applications may require several types of terminals, various computers, and many users across the country. The objectives for simpler applications are naturally easier to establish than for complex ones. As applications become more complex, conflicting objectives may increase in their impact, and so more detailed objectives may be appropriate. Applications may also either depend more on the use of existing or planned terminal equipment or require special terminals. If many new terminals are required, such as in a distributed system, the time span between the conception and the acceptance of the application may be several years, during which management requirements may change.

The success of any application large or small, depends on two requisites: the manager's clear definition of needs, and the data processing (DP) expert's understanding not only of these needs but also of appropriate data processing techniques. The range of expertise required for success calls for a joint effort by the user-manager and a DP expert. While the user-manager must provide overall direction and definitions, the DP expert must understand data processing technology, and both parties must cooperate in translating management objectives into a workable data processing application.

This chapter describes the initial steps common to planning any application using either in-house, time-share, or service bureau facilities. The first section describes the manager's role, the DP expert's role, and how their work should be documented.

## B. THE MANAGER'S ROLE

The manager's immediate task is to explain the proposed application, including all the details unique to the operation, to the DP expert. This explanation should be couched in terms of the methods presently used in doing the work, the end results currently available, the end results desired in the future, and the general objectives to be met. Preferably, the manager begins by preparing a description and an explanation of the present operations.

### 1. Automation Description

Describe what is to be automated. Explain just what the organization (unit, group, or branch) is doing now that is to be automated, that is, describe the information the organization now processes. Explain how this information is collected, recorded, analyzed, summarized, and reported. Name the people who currently perform this work, giving their job titles and their skills. Identify all the equipment presently used in this process, stating its location in the building or among buildings and floors. Collect sample copies of input documents, working papers, and final reports to show the DP expert. A short form for assembling all this basic information on current processing is shown in Figure 1-1.

FIGURE 1-1 Current Processing Practices

1. Describe current processing in general terms, explaining what functions have to be accomplished and the time allowed. Identify all people involved.

2. Provide one copy of each <u>INPUT</u> document, report, or keyed entry such as typed memo or entry on a CRT. Each copy should contain typical information.

3. Provide one copy of each <u>OUTPUT</u> document, report, or CRT screen image. List distribution of the output, and explain how distribution is determined.

4. Provide one copy of each existing computer file record and every microfilm or paper file record involved in the process. Identify records required by law, headquarters or other authority.

## 2. Current Work Explanation

Describe the end results of your current work. If you prepare a report or form, then explain:

a. the need for column headings and captions,
b. the meaning of column headings and captions,
c. the arrangement of information on the report,
d. the frequency of the report,
e. why the recipient needs the report,
f. the consequences of late reports (higher management action; loss or damage to company),
g. the number of copies prepared,
h. how copies are distributed (express mail, teletype, facsimile, remote computer printout, or other),
i. the present shortcomings in the finished report and
j. the present shortcomings in the report preparation process.

Be accurate and complete in describing these results since a minor item, if overlooked, can become an expensive roadblock to automating the application. An example of how a report may be explained is shown in Figure 1-2; which contains a detailed explanation for the heading of a report. In some cases, explanations may be limited to a few words about the headings because the application is simple and the DP expert is familiar with the manager's needs. Complex applications should be explained in more detail.

FIGURE 1-2 Report Analysis

General Instructions: Include every heading and caption. Explain every item.

EXAMPLE 1 - HEADINGS

(DATE)

WEEKLY SALES ANALYSIS
NY REGIONAL OFFICE

- - - - - - - - - - - - - - - - - - - - - - - - - - - - - - - -

EXPLANATION:

(DATE) is the date of the report preparation in the form of MONTH, DAY, YEAR. The month is a three-letter abbreviation and the day and year are two-digit numbers. The report is distributed to twelve executives and referred to frequently over a period of at least six months. Some of the executives are in the Midwest.

The second date identifies the sales week being reported. Normally the report is prepared within three days after the end of the sales week (Sunday midnight), but it may be delayed several days during holiday seasons.

- - - - - - - - - - - - - - - - - - - - - - - - - - - - - - - -

(TITLE) The NY REGIONAL OFFICE report includes NY city, plus three counties, one in New Jersey. There are sixty-four regional office reports which must be prepared weekly.

The present title is satisfactory to executives who have been with the company for a long time, because they know the counties and areas involved. However, the title is often misread by executives who use the reports occasionally. The names of all counties and cities involved should be added to the report to avoid this confusion. Statistical studies using these reports are prone to error, since sales areas covered by the report change from time to time.

## 3. Administrative Data Requirements

If a large DP organization or an obviously complex application is involved, you must supply much more information, including related administrative data. This information will help identify and coordinate initial, later, more comprehensive documentation. The necessary administrative data is presented in Figure 1-3. Seven items of information should always be provided:

a. The Project Title establishes a common identification for the proposed computer application.
b. The Requesting Organization information establishes responsibility.
c. The Date of the Request establishes priority for the DP advisor.
d. The Principal Project Contact's Name is useful when action parties may be changed during the course of development or when the application development process involves a number of people who must coordinate their work.
e. The Type of Request categorizes the proposed effort.
f. The Required Completion Date and an explanation are desirable information, since slight changes in timing could be important to both the user-manager and the DP expert.
g. The list under Documentation Supplied identifies important reference documents.

FIGURE 1-3 Administrative Data for Data Processing Requests

1. Project Title/Name
   Include abbreviation, if any.
   Include control or reference number, if any.
   Include accounting charge number, billing code.

2. Name of the Requesting Organization

3. Date of Request

4. Principal Project Contact Name, Telephone Number, and Office Location.
   Give alternate contact, if any.

5. Type (Classification) of Request (new application, revision, modification, report preparation)

6. Required Completion Date
   Explain basis for selecting this date.

7. Documentation Supplied
   List all documents and materials supplied.
   If many items are involved, identify each with a letter or number, so that they may be easily recognized.
   Classify them as "Summary" and "Detail" materials.

## 4. Objectives Description

Describe in both general and specific terms, the objectives you wish to achieve and the methods to follow in successfully automating the application. This statement helps direct the DP expert's job.

Your objectives should specify cost or level of effort limits, time schedules, allowable operational changes, ease of future modifications and expansion, and extent of security and reliability. General objectives could include items such as:

a. cost reduction (how much),
b. cost control (where, who applies),
c. increased sales (which product, what time period involved, how much in dollars or percentages),
d. improved product quality (state measure of quality and amount of improvement desired),
e. reduced use of raw material (state material, such as, electrical power, steel ingots, clerical hours to process a hundred claims; quantify reduction in pounds, tons, hours, square feet, and so on; and specify time period to reach this goal).

More specific goals should reflect improvement in location, timeliness, form or quality of information. Identify and explain controlling factors. Specific goals could include items such as:

a. provide sales reports two days sooner,
b. provide credit information on customers within ten seconds on 95 percent of all telephone orders,
c. provide a revised manufacturing schedule by 7:00 a.m. daily,
d. collect sales information from field locations, and provide summaries by product line at the home office every morning,
e. provide a statement of cash balances at 9:00 a.m. daily, with data received up to 6:00 p.m. the previous night,
f. provide a weekly count of personnel, including offers outstanding and anticipated openings,
g. utilize existing terminal equipment,
h. fit new equipment into the same space or less,
i. operate terminals in the current manufacturing environment (withstand dust, noise),
j. have equipment operational 99 percent of the required time,
k. limit operator access to information on a

terminal (four levels of passwords are used on terminals, and terminals in the factory have hardware restrictions to prevent reading confidential information),

l. allow system expansion to serve regional sales offices by simply adding equipment,

m. provide system capable of processing a 50-percent increase in transactions without excessive delay in response (the delay will not exceed five seconds 95 percent of the time),

n. insure that system expansion will require minimal changes in computer software (Two to four hours programming work in updating a list of terminals, authorized users, or such).

Preparing a complete, accurate, and detailed list of specific goals to support the more general objectives is often difficult. Setting goals that cannot be met reflects poorly on the manager involved. Setting nominal goals suggests that higher-level managers are not aware of what is actually occurring in their function. Higher-level management is usually apprehensive if unrealistic or trivial goals are proposed. A careful combination of adequately defined, reasonable goals helps the DP application meet all objectives. If the list of goals is vague or incomplete, the DP application may meet the goals yet be partially or totally unacceptable. This list of goals will be needed later in the application process as part of the formal documentation between the user-manager and the DP function.

## C. THE DP ROLE IN ESTABLISHING APPLICATIONS

The DP expert's role is to change the way the work is performed with a minimum of disruption and expense. As a practical matter, the DP expert should try to avoid obtaining new equipment, minimize training required by operators and users, shun radically new software that has not been fully proven, rigidly test each new or revised application before turning it over to the customer, and implement all systems in small digestible steps. In short, the expert must promote change, both at a price and at a rate that the user-manager is willing and able to pay, and in a way that gains positive acceptance by the affected user staff. To promote change within budget, you must continually estimate and reevaluate the proposed costs and cost alternatives, as well as recognize and weigh the intangible advantages and deficiencies.

The DP expert may have inherent limitations in effectiveness. Although the expert may possess an impressive background in data processing, that background may not include all technical aspects of the proposed application, nor involve extensive experience in the user's business. This limited background is frequently discussed in DP trade publications and conferences but is not brought to the attention of potential users. Even if the DP expert is in the user's business, the user must give specific management direction. Giving carte blanche, instead of specific instruction, leaves many questions unanswered on how to perform the work and how to approach project choices along the way. Such lack of direction often leads to cost overruns, delays, and a poorly fitting application.

## 1. Equipment Review

Review and check available DP equipment for possible use in the proposed new system. Check such items as:

a. condition: age, operational status, maintenance required, availability of maintenance, reliability, and
b. use: available capacity, options that may be added or modified, operation knowledge, present and potential effectiveness, location, and portability.

On occasion, making improvements in the present equipment will avoid the need for a new application system. In many instances, improvements will relieve the presure for immediate installation of a new application, allowing more time to do the proposed job and reducing costs. At other times, equipment from another room or office may be used on a part-time basis to improve current operations. Other suggestions for upgrading present equipment include:

* increasing terminal speed on typewriter-style equipment from 15 characters per second (cps) to 30 or 45 cps,
* reassigning equipment to more important functions,
* adding auxiliary printers to a terminal,
* adding a second screen to an existing cathode

ray tube (CRT) device, so that messages on the one CRT may be seen immediately by other office or factory personnel.

Depending upon objectives, it may be easy to add new slow speed typewriter terminals or add optional features to existing terminals. High-speed printers with screens, stylized input codes, passwords, and preprinted forms may be too complex, although more effective. In summary, upgrading and improvement steps should be consistent with meeting the detailed goals and objectives established by the user-management.

**2. Use of Systems Software**

Systems software in an existing local computer system may have features that are not being fully employed in the user's current DP application. New systems software, installed on the computer after the original application was designed, often has added features that could be used. Improved control of terminal access could improve the security of information. More comprehensive audit trails and recovery procedures would improve reliability. Adopting new software may improve an existing application, thus avoiding the costs and delays associated with a new application. Additional systems software changes may speed processing, if corresponding changes are made in the existing application.

**3. Packaged Computer Software**

Special computer applications software "packages" may be available in the local computer center for financial modeling, report printing and reformatting (such as MARK IV), statistical analysis (SAS), and for other purposes. Even if these special packages have been used on an existing application, an updated version may be available that has features that can be used to improve the current computer application. When a totally new application is required, software available at the local computer center, from an outside vendor, or from a service bureau may have many of the needed capabilities. Normally, the DP expert can advise the user of the opportunities to use these packages.

## D. DOCUMENTING THE APPLICATION

A proposed computer application should be adequately documented. In practice, "adequate" means as little as necessary to insure satisfactory end results. Faulty documentation means that the material is incomplete, not what was wanted, or hard to use and perhaps ambiguous. Documentation requirements must be established, the information must be organized, and the material should be prepared in an easily usable format.

### 1. Establishing Documentation Requirements

From a manager's viewpoint, good documentation is complete, thorough, and accurate without redundancy and unanswered questions. To be "good," it must contain all pertinent information, should be easy to read, and must be understandable by all the people who will have to use it. Since documentation is expensive and time-consuming to produce, a manager should minimize the amount required. The actual quantity needed depends on the size and complexity of the application, and ranges from a few pages to several hundred. Good documentation:

a. Provides technical information to allow a manager to determine that an application is being developed effectively. At each point where resources must be committed, the manager should be able to review progress and determine whether further planned expenditures and projected completion dates are reasonable and cost-effective. The manager must be given enough information to determine if changes in budget, schedule, or objectives are needed and justifiable.
b. Records technical information needed to direct the continued development and implementation of the application.
c. Establishes a common basis for users and data processing people to manage the application development, as well as to operate the completed application.
d. Informs other parties, such as higher management and managers in sister divisions, how the application will operate in practice, so that they can recognize the potential benefits of the application and can share in using or supporting the application.

### 2. Organizing The Documentation

In establishing an application, the manager may

conveniently organize the required documentation into as many as five document types. Large applications will require that these documents be filled out in detail. Smaller applications can often be adequately supported with much less information, and may frequently combine several types of documents. The two types of documents that record objectives and define the application are:

a. The Project Application Request, which is normally prepared by the user-manager who needs to automate.
b. The Feasibility Study, which is prepared as a joint effort between the user-manager and the DP function.

Many of the more technical details in the documentation will be prepared by the DP function after discussion with the user. Actual preparation effort reflects the manpower available to each organization, as well as the degree of importance attached to the documentation by each party.

The Project Request is the official request by the user-manager to DP to begin an automation project. This request is outlined in Figure 1-4. The formal Project Request is comprised of three major sections: Administrative Information, Project Description, and Data Processing Status.

The Administrative Information section is a direct expansion of the general administrative information described previously in Figure 1-3, Administrative Data for Data Processing Requests. The administrative information includes approval, identification, and priority information.

The Project Description has four parts:

a. It explains the objectives of the proposed computer application.
b. It describes the service requested.
c. It identifies all organizations affected by the new application (branches, groups in the company).
d. It describes other related projects or applications.

The last part of the Project Request, called DP Status, allows the data processing function to record the status of the request.

The Feasibility Study is a document that provides an analysis of objectives, requirements, and

FIGURE 1-4 Project Request

I. ADMINISTRATIVE INFORMATION

A. APPROVAL
1. Name and title of manager approving request
2. Date of Approval.
3. Account to be Charged
4. Name and Title of User technical contact (if not manager above)

B. IDENTIFICATION
1. Project Title/Name (include abbreviation if any)
2. Control or Reference Number
3. Name of Requesting Organization
4. Principal Project Contact (include name, title, telephone number and office location)
5. Date of request Preparation
6. Type of request (classify request, such as new application, development, revision or modification of existing application, ADP Report design, ADP Survey)

C. PRIORITY
1. Completion Date Desired (explain why this date set)
2. Latest Completion Date (point out major business disaster or loss if task not completed by this date)
3. Priority Relative to Other Requests (If there are other existing requests for service by your office, state the priority this request should receive relative to others. If overtime or an outside contractor may be allowed in order to meet schedules, explain.)

II. PROJECT DESCRIPTION

A. OBJECTIVES
1. General end objectives of this application (state completion date, security, training)
2. Objectives to be met in performance (state funds available, frequency and nature of progress reports)

B. SERVICE REQUESTED
1. Functions to Be Performed
2. Outputs Expected
3. Inputs Available

FIGURE 1-4 (continued)

C. ORGANIZATIONS AFFECTED (if any)
   1. Identify other organization/groups which are affected by the timely completion or proper performance of this proposed application.
   2. Explain effects

D. RELATED WORK (if any)
   1. Identify other projects/applications to which this request relates
   2. Specify common/overlapping inputs, outputs, and/or processes with related projects/applications
   3. Provide reference memos and documents

III. DP STATUS

A. Date Received by DP Function

B. DP Action Party Assigned (name, telephone number, title, location)

C. DP Project Code(s) Assigned

D. Date DP Project Plan and Cost Estimate Prepared

E. Pertinent DP Standards and Procedures

F. Date DP Official Reply to User

systems concepts, an evaluation of alternative approaches to meet the objectives, and an identification of a proposed approach. This document is outlined in Figure 1-5. A Feasibility Study differs in size and scope according to the application and the size and nature of the company involved. The study is typically prepared in two sections. The first section, called General, includes administrative information that ties it to the previous Project Request (Figure 1-4) and contains a management summary of the study.

The second section, called Technical Analysis, reports the technical analysis of the proposed computer application in five subsections. If there is an existing computer application involved, it is described in the first subsection. The other subsections are used for a description of application requirements, alternative application designs, overall impacts of the proposed application, and schedule information.

FIGURE 1-5 Feasibility Study

I. GENERAL

A. INTRODUCTION

1. Give name and identification of the proposed application.
2. Give names of user manager, DP action party, computer center inhouse, other company location, outside service bureau).
3. Summarize system outputs, inputs and processing required.

B. MANAGEMENT SUMMARY

1. State the specific requirements this application will meet. Describe the new service, increased capacity, or improvement expected in current service.
2. Describe the major objectives to be met by the application, including specific amounts of cost saving, manpower reduction, increased production, increased speed in processing, improved information for decision making, compliance with law or regulation.
3. State assumptions made in determining feasibility of this application, including time and dollar budgets, availability of existing and new hardware, costs for data communications, programmer availability, completion of related projects.
4. Describe how the technical analysis was performed. If modeling, benchmarking, or simulation was used, explain why and give results. Explain the basis for arriving at the recommended system (cost, met time limit, ease of use).
5. List alternatives considered, explaining why the preferred solution was selected and why other alternatives were rejected.

II. TECHNICAL ANALYSIS

A. ANALYSIS OF PRESENT SYSTEM (If existing application)
   1. Prepare an overall logical block diagram to summarize the existing system used for meeting the application.
   2. Identify personnel, equipment and facilities now required.
   3. Specify workload processed by the existing system, and costs incurred for personnel, equipment, facilities and overhead.

FIGURE 1-5 (continued)

B. APPLICATION REQUIREMENTS
1. Describe outputs (reports on CRT screens, printed documents) in terms of frequency prepared or used, distribution, and information content. Attach copies of typical output reports.
2. Describe inputs (data from existing computer tapes, data collection forms, reports inputted via telecommunications systems) in terms of their source, type, volume, format, and frequency of receipt.
3. Describe all files. Identify each item of information in a record within the file. Explain the use of each file and the frequency of file updating.
4. Prepare an overall logical (block) diagram, as well as more detail flow charts to summarize the required processing.
5. Describe any special needs for data security, control of transactions, information storage and retrieval, or interface to existing applications.

C. ALTERNATIVE APPLICATION DESIGN
1. Describe each major alternative technical approach to the proposed application.
2. Explain the basis for selecting the proposed application concept. (NOTE: Small applications do not need lengthy discussions.)

D. PROPOSED APPLICATION
1. Describe the overall concept and how it meets the application requirements and the management objectives.
2. Describe anticipated operational impacts of this application including:
   a. new and changed equipment and physical facilities,
   b. changes in software in related applications,
   c. organization, personnel, and skill requirement changes,
   d. changes in user and DP center procedures,
   e. data entry and output reporting procedures and schedules.
3. Describe anticipated implementation impacts including:
   a. work to be performed by the user,
   b. work to be performed by the DP center,

FIGURE 1-5 (continued)

c. work to be performed by others via contract or request by user and/or the DP center.

4. Describe major factors that may influence the completion time schedule, the budget for development, and future time cost in the proposed application.

E. PROPOSED SCHEDULE

1. List major milestones.
2. Identify each point at which the user and/or the DP center must or can make major decisions to change the project schedule or cost.

## E. SUMMARY

Application objectives and application requirements must be defined by the manager to the DP expert to get cost-effective applications. If these steps are not followed, delays, cost overruns, and poorly fitting applications may result. Computer expertise is helpful to the manager in explaining what is needed. However, uncomplicated documentation formats and procedures will reduce this need.

First, describe current processing practices. Second, consider how existing reports must be analyzed, so that future automated versions will be satisfactory. Third, prepare a list of objectives. These materials and all other documentation should fit together as complete and understandable. Part of this coordination is reflected in the use of basic administrative data which appears in each document. Next, prepare a Project Request. Then, work with the appropriate DP expert to perform and document a Feasibility Study. This study relates technical feasibility and choices in implementation to the objectives and to specific costs, benefits, and proposed time schedules.

# 2

# Evaluating alternative solutions

## A. INTRODUCTION

Solutions to DP problems may vary from simple to complex. Obvious factors, such as expected project costs and time schedules, may be misleading guides to use in picking the best solutions. This chapter discusses the overall corporate setting in which evaluation takes place, explains the concepts used to select the best solutions, and describes the information needed in the decision-making process.

## B. EVALUATION CONCEPTS

An evaluation of alternatives should conform to general corporate policies, as well as follow a reasonable logical procedure. When properly performed, the total evaluation process is easily explained, and it justifies the selection of a specific alternative. Inadequate facts are discovered early in the process, minimizing ill-founded and arbitrary judgments. These same policies and concepts apply during the process of implementing the approved solution. The corporate policies and concepts include:

1. meeting corporate requirements,
2. supporting management objectives,
3. determining costs,
4. weighing intangibles,
5. measuring benefits,
6. adjusting for the time value of money,
7. establishing a return on investment,
8. analyzing tax effects, and
9. defining effectiveness.

## 1. Meeting Corporate Requirements

Major projects require funding, as well as a commitment of management personnel. As a result, corporations normally establish policy regarding:

a. the standard methods for analyzing and establishing costs and benefits of alternative investments, and
b. the minimum financial thresholds that any investment must meet for consideration.

Corporate policy will normally require that all pertinent factors be included in performing an evaluation. Specify in detailed rules the minimum set of factors that must be included, and the method of preparing a comparison between alternative proposals and adjusting factors, so that the final comparisons will not be distorted or misleading. Explain to similar depth the major items of cost in each alternative proposal. Cost factors to be included may be specified or suggested in the corporate policy statement itself, or in an attached or referenced detail procedure or forms.

Factors commonly specified as costs include:

a. building and facilities,
b. ADP equipment,
c. ADP software,
d. data communications equipment and services,
e. supplies and utilities, and
f. personnel.

You may provide similar list of cost savings and a listing of intangible benefits as shown in Figure 2-8.

Labor costs and assumptions regarding changes

in labor costs should be reasonable, and should be developed in the same manner for all estimates that are to be compared with each other. Often construction of new buildings and facilities is a significant part of the projected costs. In these instances, estimated construction cost should be prepared with special care. If a contractor's estimate is secured, it should be based upon reasonable detailed specifications. Costs should reflect a contractor's current estimate for facility construction, rather than reflect an estimate drawn from an apparently similar project. This apparently similar project might be very different because it was built in another part of the country, or was constructed to meet different management objectives, such as physical security. Possible increases in cost due to inflation should be noted in analyzing each alternative.

## 2. Supporting Management Objectives

The solution chosen should support operational management objectives. The first step in supporting these objectives is to list management objectives and rank the objectives in terms of importance. Objectives that frequently appear on such a list include:

a. utilize existing equipment,
b. minimize training needed,
c. meet desired time schedules,
d. stay within budget,
e. allow for future improvements without requiring major redo of the application, and
f. perform with high reliability.

In reviewing the alternative solutions, the manager should begin by looking for management objectives that are not met. This approach will eliminate some apparently desirable solutions that clearly do not meet the required objectives, as well as force reconsideration of the objectives. Vaguely worded or missing objectives will become apparent, so that they may be more clearly stated, or added to the list while they can still affect decision-making.

Each alternative solution may satisfy one or several objectives, but rarely all. One alternative may meet the required performance level, but only through the use of elaborate new equipment, extensive training, and a large budget. Another alternative may provide a less than optimum level of performance, but may reduce budget costs to an acceptable level. If budget cost control is a principal objective, this second alternative may be preferred over the first. Still another alternative may meet budget and time schedules, but it may provide only a small initial improvement in performance. The most desirable alternative is frequently a compromise that meets some objectives completely and other objectives in part. Only the user can judge which compromise solution is best for the organization. When a number of alternatives are to be considered or when a number of individuals are involved in the decision-making process, the evaluation is complicated and prone to delay. The evaluation choices are more easily compared and understood by all if the information can be assembled in a matrix form, as illustrated in Figure 2-1. The sample data in this matrix illustrates this difficulty, and emphasizes the need to list all objectives and to rate their relative importance in supporting management objectives.

FIGURE 2-1 Alternative Evaluation Matrix
(All Data for Illustration Only)

| | | Objectives to Meet | | | | | | | | | |
|---|---|---|---|---|---|---|---|---|---|---|---|
| | | | | | | Training Required | | | | | |
| | | | | Completion | | On the Job | | Outside | | | |
| | | Interferes with current | Budget Objective | 9/15 | 11/30 | 4hr | 20hr | 2da | +2da | | |
| | Alternative | Operation | $ 100,000 | Best | Must | Best | Good | OK | Poor | Reliable | Results |
| 1. | New equip and procedures required. | No Parallel Operation | $150,000 | No | 90% | | | | Yes | Excel | Excel |
| 2. | Some equip and procedure change. | Little Parallel Operation | $100,000 | No | 100% | | Yes | | | Excel | Good |
| 3. | Minor equip and procedure changes. | Some 3 mo. cutover | $ 25,000 | Yes | Yes | Yes | | | | Poor | Fair |
| 4. | Same equipment. Procedure and facility changes. | Yes Cutover in 4 stages 6 mo. min. | $ 25,000 | Yes | Yes | | | Yes | | Good | Fair |

## 3. Determining Costs

The normal process of managing any business includes accounting for sales, inventory, accounts receivable and payable, payrolls, and the like. Formal accounting records must be prepared according to generally recognized accounting principles, and to meet business needs, as well as legal requirements. These accounting records are the starting point for determining what costs are actually changed if a specific alternative is chosen.

Normal accounting practices for a capital asset often cause a manager to make incorrect judgments about costs that will be incurred or saved by selecting a specific alternative. Costs incurred with a specific application will include hardware-related items, as well as application-unique costs. Accounting costs for installing computer equipment include:

a. purchase cost of hardware,
b. purchase cost of software (programs, manuals, hardware documentation), and
c. installation, test, and modification of the systems software (operating/executive system).

Hardware installation and related software change may be important factors. Physical installation costs include an allocation of the cost of plant maintenance personnel; for instance, if plant maintenance charges $20 per hour and 100 hours are needed for such tasks as wiring, moving other equipment, installing new hardware, then $2,000 will be charged. The systems software that comes with the new hardware must be installed, tested, and often modified by the existing inhouse DP staff. Their salary costs will be added to the total accounting costs for the computer equipment.

Some of the application-unique costs are for DP personnel to do applications systems design and programming work. Maintenance people, as well as the inhouse DP people, will continue to receive their salaries even if the application is never installed. Company overhead will also continue. These costs are simply a redistribution of existing costs and do not require additional dollars. Other costs will actually increase or be reduced because of the application. In making a decision to install a specific DP application, compare these additional out-of-pocket costs and actual dollars saved.

## 4. Weighing Intangibles

Intangible factors cannot be ignored in evaluating an alternative. In some instances these factors may be the deciding items in selecting a specific computer application solution. Major intangibles to be reviewed include:

a. employee attitudes,
b. viewpoints of outsiders, and
c. value of advanced technology with uncertain future costs and benefits.

Employee attitudes are frequently a crucial factor. Installing a particular alternative may require personnel reassignment, changes in size and use of physical space, and changes in many familiar working routines. Such changes may cause some employees to worry about the loss of their job, the reduced promotional opportunity, the inability to learn new technology, and similar things. Time previously spent in productive work tends to be spent in unproductive worry. A specific application solution may allow minor existing procedures to continue unchanged, and thus reduce the disruption and worry. Physical rearrangement of employees may be accomplished with a minimum of hurt feelings and with positive acceptance, if it is identified as part of management's plan to provide more comfortable working conditions, rather than as an apparently arbitrary and thoughtless action. Positive employee cooperation may be a highly critical factor in a successful computer application, especially when unions are involved or when present labor-management relations are hostile. Many employees will not realize benefits of change until the new application has been put into operation and obvious results appear, such as:

a. reduction in physical labor,
b. elimination of repetitious clerical checking and filing, and
c. fewer customer complaints.

Another intangible factor is the viewpoint and attitude that outside customers, major suppliers, and lending institutions will take. The computer application may help to convince them that for example, the company intends to remain in business, is improving its service to customers, will be able to reduce inventories, and will be more profitable. Influencing such opinions may be significant in evaluating the relative merits of a specific alternative for a computer application.

Use of advanced technology may expose the planned application to an unknown risk of delay or failure. At the same time, use of the specific technology may have advantages, such as less time required and lower costs for long distance telephone lines. A hardware improvement might allow the computer application to run more quickly because of faster movement of information to and from disk storage. But this same advantage might also cause timing problems in which other pieces of hardware do not always maintain sufficient speed to avoid occasional serious failure. There is no way to eliminate completely the possible adverse effects, just as some of the benefits of higher internal operating speeds cannot be given a dollar equivalent.

## 5. Measuring Benefits

The benefits of a computer application are many, and may be difficult to translate into dollar terms. These benefits reflect improvements in information timelines, format, and location. Common examples of these benefits and their measurement include such items as:

a. information available sooner
--allows accounts receivables to be collected faster, thereby reducing the size and cost of short term bank loans (measure the interest savings),
--allows discount to be taken on purchases (measure the amount of discounts taken due to having this info),
--allows slow-selling fashion merchandise to be identified quickly, so that reorders may be cancelled (estimate the loss, if merchandise had been received)
--allows persistent failures in a product to be identified, so that manufacturing changes may be made (identify the warranty repair cost avoided, estimate court suit cost avoided,

b. information format improved
--rearranges information and highlights critical data for immediate action; for instance, provides accounts receivable data in terms of dollar size, time overdue, and such (measure loss avoided on further credit extension, measure profit gained by selling to acceptable customer otherwise not shipped),
--lists hospital or wholesalers' drug inventories in terms of drug life, to avoid loss

due to drugs becoming outdated (measure loss under previous system),

c. information better located
--provides manufacturing plants with daily changes in production schedules to prevent buildup of stock (measure cost of stock build-up under previous system),
--provides sales offices with inventory available at remote locations to avoid loss of customer orders, as well as unnecessary shipping (measure profit gained on orders, savings on shipping),
--gives corporate treasurer information on foreign exchange rates to enable obtaining best rates (measure by multiplying difference between current and previous rate dollars involved).

These examples show that the benefit must be transformed into an equivalent that can be measured in dollars. The process is rarely easy and requires a familiarity with the business, as well as a financial analysis background.

## 6. Adjusting for the Time Value of Money

Alternative computer application solutions often have different sets of costs and benefits. The costs incurred and the rate at which dollar benefits are received may differ considerably from one solution to another. Costs and benefits involved in a specific computer application may also vary from one year to the next. In addition, a dollar in hand today is a certain item, while a dollar promised for next year is uncertain. From an acounting standpoint, total costs are divided by the expected life of an application to give an annual cost. Benefits may be summed up, and then divided by the total number of years available to give an average benefit per year.

To compare the costs of one alternative with another requires more than simple comparison of total or average cost and benefits in the two alternatives. A dollar today differs from a dollar in the future, because interest could be earned on today's dollar while waiting for the future. This interest earning must be taken into consideration. One of the best commonly used methods to do this is known as discounted present value analysis. The technique can and should be used with both costs and benefits over the life of the application. To compare costs (or benefits) over time, the stream of future dollars involved is discounted to reflect the equivalent sum of current present-day dollars. If we assume a 10-percent interest rate is involved, $110 next year would be exactly equal to $100 today. On this basis, future dollars may be equated to present dollars, as illustrated in Figure 2-2.

FIGURE 2-2 Comparing Present and Future Dollars*

| Year | Equivalent Present Dollars (discounted) | Future Dollars | Accounting Dollar Values |
|---|---|---|---|
| Now | $100 | $ - | $100 |
| +1 | 100 | 110 | 110 |
| +2 | 100 | 121 | 121 |
| +3 | 100 | 133 | 133 |
| +4 | 100 | 146 | 146 |
| | $500 | | $610 |

*A 10% interest rate is used.
Calculations are rounded for convenience.

Figure 2-2 shows that a five-year project with an accounting cost of $610 has a discounted present cost of $500.

If the costs of a solution are concentrated in the earlier (or later) years of one alternative, in comparison to another, apparently equal acounting costs represent very different real costs. Figure 2-3 illustrates this difference using a discount rate of 10 percent for comparing two alternative solutions over a period of five years. In Figure 2-3, the two alternatives have different expenditure patterns, although the accounting costs are the same. When discounting is applied, the costs of alternative one appear much larger than alternative two.

FIGURE 2-3 Comparing the Costs of Two Alternatives Using Discounted Present Value Analysis

| | ALTERNATIVE 1 | | ALTERNATIVE 2 | |
|---|---|---|---|---|
| Year | Discounted $ | Accounting $ | Discounted $ | Accounting $ |
| 0 | $ 1,100 | $ 1,100 | $ 100 | $ 100 |
| 1 | 91 | 100 | 91 | 100 |
| 2 | 82 | 100 | 82 | 100 |
| 3 | 74 | 100 | 296 | 400 |
| 4 | 67 | 100 | 536 | 800 |
| | $ 1,414 | $ 1,500 | $ 1,105 | $ 1,500 |

Source: All figures are for illustration only.

The same technique of discounting dollars is used to analyze the value of benefits to be received over a period of time. Discounting should be used to compare the costs of two or more alternative applications. Discounting is also used to compare the costs versus the benefits for a single application. Figure 2-4 illustrates the analysis of a specific application using assumptions that are considered common. In Figure 2-4, we assume the following:

a. A discount rate of 15 percent is to be used as set by the Corporate Controller.

b. The useful life of the application is set at five years, reflecting the decision of the responsible operating manager. This useful life period has subsequently received the concurrence of the Vice President of the division.

c. The Corporation requires a minimum 25 percent return on investment to consider a project. Projects returning over 50 percent are considered very desirable. Projects returning over 75 percent are considered of maximum importance.

FIGURE 2-4 Comparing Costs and Benefits on a Specific Application Using Discounted Present Value Analysis

| Year | Cost | Discounted | Benefits | Discounted |
|---|---|---|---|---|
| 0 | $40,000 | $40,000 | $ 20,000 | $20,000 |
| 1 | 10,000 | 8,500 | 20,000 | 17,000 |
| 2 | 2,000 | 1,445 | 20,000 | 14,450 |
| 3 | 2,000 | 1,228 | 20,000 | 12,283 |
| 4 | 2,000 | 1,004 | 20,000 | 10,440 |
| 5 | 2,000 | 887 | 20,000 | 8,874 |
| | $58,000 | $53,104 | $120,000 | $83,047 |

Discounted Rate of Return = 83,047/53,104 = 56.4%
Accounting Rate of Return = 120,000/58,000 = 106.9%

Source: Figures are for illustration only.
Note: The cost and benefit values each year are assumed. Figures are rounded off for convenience.

Financial evaluation should always use a discounted present value approach or an equivalent. Often practical problems in applying present value analysis result in not using the technique. These problems include:

a. agreeing upon a reasonable discount rate such as 10 percent, 15 percent or 20 percent,
b. agreeing upon the values that will occur in future years (costs to maintain the new applications software),
c. having sufficient technical knowledge to identify and include all the important factors in the financial analysis (since a change in the proposed terminal locations may expose the equipment to unauthorized users, what costs should be estimated for protecting the equipment?).

After performing this analysis, we can conclude that the proposed application is a highly desirable use of funds, because it will result in a 56.4-percent return on investment.

Additional techniques in financial analysis may be employed by some organizations and are typically performed by the Comptroller's or Treasurer's office.

## 7. Establishing a Return on Investment

Money costs. The dollars requested for a proposed computer application could be invested in other uses. These dollars are worth at least the interest they could earn. If the corporation has bank loans or bonds outstanding, the dollars are worth the interest rate, plus the corporations's administrative cost in negotiating and managing the debt. A proposed investment that returns 10 percent is financially unsatisfactory, if the corporation cost of money is nearer 20 percent. As a result, corporate policies are issued establishing conditions to be met if a major investment is to be made. Policies commonly appear as rules governing the minimum acceptable rate of return and the time period to be considered in calculating the return. A specific rule may state that if a proposed new use of capital funds cannot return at least 25 percent over its minimum useful life, then it will not be considered. This return on investment may be stated as a specific numeric value or may be a percentage to be added to the corporation's cost of capital. Thus, if the current cost of long term capital funds is 15 percent and the add-on percentage is 10 percent, the project must return 25 percent more to be considered.

Investment alternatives may have different useful lives. A highly tailored DP application may be very efficient, but is likely to require major revision and have a shorter life than a more general DP application. A simple solution may have low costs, but be reasonably effective for only a few years.

In traditional analysis of costs and benefits, physical equipment is a large part of the cost, and even though the specific application no longer has useful life, the equipment itself may have a significant residual value. Residual value is clearly a reduction in the costs of the application. Residual value can be easily acounted for by being treated as a reduction in cost at the end of the application's life. However, determining the dollar value to assign is difficult, since many changes may occur over the life of the application.

Corporate return on investment standards have often been established and used for a period of years. Frequently, the standard adopted includes little or no compensation for high rates of inflation. In fact, if the planned application was to be implemented in an inflation-ridden South American country, the investment cost calculations may be subject to additional revision for inflation impact. This inflation adjustment may be highly significant, as shown in Figure 2-5.

FIGURE 2-5 Inflation Impact Calculations

| | Beginning of Year | +1 Year | Totals |
|---|---|---|---|
| Investment Cost | $100,000 | $ | $ |
| Inflation Factor 12% | | 12,000 | -12,000 |
| Interest @ 18% | | 18,000 | +18,000 |
| Tax Saving on Interest | | 9,000 | - 9,000 |
| Net Cost of $100,000 Investment | | | $- 3,000 |

Assumptions:

1. Analysis is for one year only. Presumably these calculations could be extended to future years for an application with a useful life of more than one year.
2. Rates for interest and inflation are assumed.
3. If the application were made in a foreign country, interest expenses would have to be similarly deductible.

Inflation effectively increases the value of an investment. This increase in value, plus the savings in taxes, offset the interest cost in Figure 2-5 and suggest reconsideration of a 25-percent return-on-investment standard. Reevaluation of such a standard is normally within the scope of the financial function.

Frequently a proposed computer application is planned to take advantage of equipment that is already available for other applications. In such instances, costs arise primarily from paying programmer and analyst salaries, training users, publishing operating instructions and users' manuals, and using computer time to develop and check out the new application. If such an application becomes obsolete, much of the application documentation, computer programs, and user training has no further value. In this instance, residual value will be low or nonexistent.

## 8. Analyzing Tax Effects

Taxes have a significant impact on evaluating the financial desirability of alternative DP applications. Computer applications with the same gross rate of return may have different returns after tax effects.

In general, if costs of an application can be amortized over a short time period, such as three years, the immediate and near future after-tax dollar costs are substantially less than the before-tax costs. In many applications, the cost components involved are depreciated or expensed over different time periods. When a specific computer application may be immediately expensed, these costs reduce corporate profits, which would otherwise be taxed at approximately a 50-percent tax rate. Thus, a $25,000 computer application that could be expensed in the year the application is implemented would cost the corporation only $12,500. The actual savings on taxes otherwise paid reflects the specific application of tax laws on the corporation. Small corporations may be subject only to the minimum tax rates of approximately 20 percent, while other corporations may have large depletion allowances or have credits reflecting the impact of foreign tax laws. From a tax standpoint, it make sense to charge expense to reduce taxes paid now, and hopefully obtain the benefits in later years, if a lower tax rate is expected. Figure 2-6 illustrates this tax planning when it is expected that high tax rates for several years will be followed by lower rates---say, 50 percent now and 30 percent later.

In this instance, the effect of taxes is quite significant since the return on investment after taxes is 76 percent and, per Figure 2-4, we consider any return 75 percent or larger to be extremely desirable.

FIGURE 2-6 Discounted Present Value Analysis
Adjusted for Changing Tax Rates

| Year | Cost | After-Tax Discounted | Tax% | Cost | Benefits | After-Tax Discounted | Tax% | Benefit |
|---|---|---|---|---|---|---|---|---|
| 0 | $40,000 | $40,000 | 50 | $20,000 | $ 20,000 | $20,000 | 50 | $10,000 |
| 1 | 10,000 | 8,500 | 50 | 4,250 | 20,000 | 17,000 | 50 | 8,500 |
| 2 | 2,000 | 1,445 | 50 | 722 | 20,000 | 14,450 | 50 | 7,225 |
| 3 | 2,000 | 1,228 | 30 | 860 | 20,000 | 12,283 | 30 | 8,596 |
| 4 | 2,000 | 1,044 | 30 | 731 | 20,000 | 10,440 | 30 | 7,308 |
| 5 | 2,000 | 887 | 30 | 621 | 20,000 | 8,874 | 30 | 6,212 |
| | $58,000 | $53,104 | | $27,184 | $120,000 | $82,047 | | $47,841 |

Discounted Rate of Return: Before Taxes 56.4%
After Taxes 76%

Source: Cost and benefit values are taken from Figure 2-4.
Tax rates are assumed for illustrative purposes only.

### 9. Defining Effectiveness

Effective use of a computer application refers to how closely the application fits actual needs. One approach provides information in a large printout at the central office. This approach may be less effective than an alternative that provides information in separate printouts distributed to the points of use. If the information changes rapidly, the printouts themselves may be continually out of date. In this instance, another alternative that provides the information as wanted on CRT screens at the points of use is more effective than either of the other choices. An illustration of this type of requirement is seen in the typical online airline reservation system. In a manufacturing organization with many widely distributed sales points, continuous communication of orders using an online system might be unduly expensive compared to a system that batched orders into headquarters several times a day. Effectiveness must be determined by the organization's needs. In practice, this means that the concerned managers reach a joint working decision on what service they will accept as effective.

## C. DOCUMENTING THE APPLICATION

Performing a careful analysis of alternatives involves obtaining considerable information, analyzing same, and organizing both the analysis process and the presentation of the conclusions. At least two types of documents are needed. These documents are the Technical Feasibility Study (discussed in Chapter 1) and the Cost/Benefit Analysis. The Cost/Benefit Analysis should be prepared with a supporting Sensitivity Analysis. This documentation provides managers with the information to continue, modify, or stop work on the proposed application.

### 1. The Cost/Benefit Analysis

The Cost/Benefit Analysis contains cost and benefit comparisons of the alternative approaches that are technically feasible. Figures 2-7 through 2-11 outline the Cost/Benefit documentation in depth. The form shown in Figure 2-7 contains pertinent general information and states the basic assumptions regarding cost factors, time schedules, and expected

FIGURE 2-7 Cost/Benefit Analysis

## I. GENERAL

A. INTRODUCTION

1. Give name and identification of the proposed application.
2. Give names of the user-manager, DP action party, computer center (inhouse, other company location, outside service bureau).
3. Summarize system outputs, inputs, and processing required.

B. MANAGEMENT SUMMARY

1. Name and describe the alternative application plans which were considered technically feasible.
2. Explain why other feasible plans were not subjected to cost/benefit analysis (if any). For example, an existing bank law forbids, special equipment cannot be obtained in sufficient time to meet a required due date, and so on.
3. State general assumptions and limitations under which this analysis was performed. For example, the C/B Analysis had to be completed within three weeks, equipment that could be considered had to be suitable to known physical hazards (operate in a dusty manufacturing environment, operate in an automobile service station, operate below ground), only domestically-produced equipment could be used, new equipment had to be compatible with existing units.
4. Describe the procedures used in conducting this analysis, the source of the basic cost/benefit information, and the techniques used in estimating and computing costs.
5. Explain the criteria used in evaluating alternatives (meeting all objectives, providing higher reliability, increasing cost effectiveness, requiring minimal physical facility changes).
6. Summarize recommendations.

## II. TECHNICAL ANALYSIS

A. CURRENT APPLICATION (if any)

1. Describe costs and benefits in terms of technical and operational characteristics.

B. ANALYSIS OF ALTERNATIVES

1. Describe the technical and operational characteristics of each alternative considered.
2. Summarize the comparative cost/benefit analysis for each alternative.

results. The first part of the format, called General, organizes general information, and the second part, called Technical Analysis, organizes technical information.

If a large application is involved, completion of the form often requires several drafts to achieve agreement among the users and DP management. The major benefit of multiple drafts is found in securing agreement and understanding among the parties. This eliminates sometimes acrimonious disputes that otherwise occur at later dates when the application is less than perfect. This information is also helpful during the implementation of the computer application as a basis for considering the extent and nature of changes that should be made in the project estimates. Figure 2-8, Comparative C/B Analysis--Summary, summarizes the detailed financial analysis.

A small application warrants minimal financial analysis effort, and may use only some of the Cost and Benefit categories shown in Figure 2-9, Comparative C/B Analysis--Application Cost--Detail, and Figure 2-10, Comparative C/B Analysis--Benefits--Detail.

Not all possible cost and benefit factors appear in these two figures, since each application is somewhat different. Some benefit factors that do not appear in these forms will not appear in any Cost or Benefit statement, since they are intangible and cannot be converted into a dollar form. Although they are intangibles, these factors may be so important as to be the determining factors in deciding to automate a requirement and in selecting a specific method of automation. All intangible factors should be listed and explained as part of the C/B analysis. Critical intangible factors normally relate to the timeliness, completeness, and organization of the data and include such items as:

a. complying with legal requirements,
b. eliminating manual drudgery,
c. ordering parts faster than previously,
d. providing more complete credit checks,
e. improving customer relations,
f. providing quicker administrative responses to employees,
g. allowing quicker revision of plans,
h. giving faster access to information, and
i. arranging information to make it easier to use.

FIGURE 2-8 Comparative C/B Analysis--Summary

| | Application Value | | |
|---|---|---|---|
| | Alternative 1 | Alternative 2 | Alternative 3 |
| Life Cost: | | | |
| Accounting | | | |
| Discounted | | | |
| Benefits: | | | |
| Accounting | | | |
| Discounted | | | |
| Accounting Payback (years) | | | |
| C/B Ration (Discounted) | | | |
| Intangible Benefits: | | | |
| Summary | | | |
| Detail | | | |

FIGURE 2-9 Comparative C/B Analysis Application Cost--Detail

| | Start-Up (Nonrecurring) Costs | Capital Investment Costs | Continuing (Recurring) Costs |
|---|---|---|---|
| **Building & Facilities** | | | |
| Acquisition & Renovation | | | |
| Environment (A/C, Power) | | | |
| Security (Fire, Police) | | | |
| **ADP Equipment** | | | |
| Processors | | | |
| Terminals | | | |
| Other | | | |
| **ADP Software** | | | |
| Purchased | | | |
| Develop | | | |
| Inhouse | | | |
| Contract | | | |
| Other | | | |
| **Data Communications** | | | |
| Equipment | | | |
| Lines | | | |
| Services | | | |
| **Supplies & Utilities** | | | |
| Supplies - ADP | | | |
| - Office | | | |
| - Other | | | |
| Utilities - Power | | | |
| - Voice Telephone | | | |
| - Other | | | |

FIGURE 2-9 (continued)

Personnel

Nonrecurring
- Planning
- Data Base Prep
- Software Conversion
- Software Studies
- Technical & Mgt Review
- Training
- Travel
- Recruitment
- Relocation
- Other

Recurring
- Salaries
- Benefits
- Training
- Travel
- Other

If an intangible benefit represents the evaluation made by another group, such as a consultant or a published source, note this fact, so that upper level management can give weight to the evaluation.

## 2. The Sensitivity Analysis

A Cost/Benefit Analysis is not complete without a supporting Sensitivity Analysis. Estimates are always uncertain. When large amounts of money are involved, every estimate is somewhat questionable. The practical question in the mind of each concerned manager is this: How reliable is the estimate? If the estimate is presented as a single set of values, the addition of an arbitrary dollar amount or the application of a set percentage factor is clearly guesswork and is likely to be only a salve to a troubled conscience. The effect of applying such an arbitrary factor is to mislead, rather than to give the user a better basis for evaluation. The estimate can be improved, however, by adding estimates for a high and a low value.

The Sensitivity Analysis is a review of the key factors developed in the Cost/Benefit Analysis to determine what changes will occur in total costs

FIGURE 2-10 Comparative C/B Analysis Benefits--Detail

| | One Time | Recurring |
|---|---|---|
| **Benefits:** | | |
| Direct Cost Savings to DP | | |
| Data Input | | |
| Processing (operating) | | |
| Raw Materials | | |
| Adm Handling | | |
| Data Storage | | |
| Central Processing Equipment | | |
| Terminals | | |
| Other Equipment | | |
| Direct Cost Savings to User | | |
| Information Processing | | |
| Reduced DP Processing Cost | | |
| Shorter Processing Cycle | | |
| Better Organized System of Reports | | |
| Improved Report Formats | | |
| Improved Information Processing | | |
| Reduced Errors | | |
| Organization Benefits | | |
| Reduce A/R Float | | |
| Obtain Prompt Payment Discount | | |
| Avoid OT by better Scheduling | | |
| Reduce out of stock cost for manufacturing or sales needs | | |
| Achieve Faster Inventory turnover | | |
| Minimize stale or obsolete stock | | |
| INTANGIBLE BENEFITS (list) | | |

(Figure 2-11) and in total benefits (Figure 2-12), if these key factors are changed. The key factors are selected according to the size and complexity of the proposed application and include such items as:

a. estimate useful life of the application (What is the possibility that a change in business will make the expected five-year life actually become four years, or will allow the application to be useful for ten years?),
b. consider workload mix, pattern and volume changes; estimate the effect on the capacity and capability of the application as now designed,
c. anticipate possible significant changes in the company structure and objectives (concentrate on consumer markets, rather than traditional industrial markets),
d. project likely changes in cost, capability, and availability of DP equipment, software, and communications (How will these changes affect the costs and benefits of the alternative applications?), and
e. review assumptions (inflation rates, alternative investments, improvements possible in existing methods, cost and time involved in training people to use the new system, employee attitudes). Consider the possible changes in these assumptions and their effect on the costs and benefits.

Estimates often have two to five key factors which comprise 80 percent of the total costs. Analyzing and predicting the high and low values likely in these components takes less effort than predicting extreme values for all components. The total estimated value can then be expanded with a probable high value and a probable low value which are realistic.

In a highly complex application alternative, probability analysis techniques may be used to develop the set of values to be assigned each key variable. Once this set of values is established, the possible changes in total costs and benefits may be evaluated.

Sensitivity Analysis is not a precise tool and should be used as an indicator of the reliability of the Cost/Benefit Analysis, rather than as a guarantee of accuracy.

FIGURE 2-11 Sensitivity Analysis--Costs

| Factor | Dollar Values: Expected | High | Low |
|---|---|---|---|
| Terminal Relocation | | | |
| Training | | | |
| Data Communications | | | |
| Salary Costs | | | |
| TOTAL | | | |

Note: Assumptions on how the high and low values have been developed, as well as an explanation of why this (or another) set of factors is used, should appear on this document or as an accompanying narrative statement.

FIGURE 2-12 Sensitivity Analysis--Benefits

| Factor | Dollar Values: Expected | High | Low |
|---|---|---|---|
| DP Savings (Itemize) | | | |
| User Savings | | | |
| DP Charges | | | |
| Personnel Cost | | | |
| Material Cost | | | |
| Other Cost | | | |
| Profit Increased | | | |
| TOTAL | | | |

Note: Assumptions on how the high and low values have been developed, as well as an explanation of why this (or another set of factors is used, should appear on this document or as an accompanying narrative statement.

## 3. Organizing The Documentation

Any manager or analyst who has managed, or participated in developing or implementing, a major computer application has been exposed to an assortment of documentation and may have considered it a necessary evil.

Much of the problem with documentation reflects poor organization of the material. Two suggested outlines for organizing documentation are shown in Figure 2-13 and 2-14. Figure 2-13 assumes a small DP application. Figure 2-14 assumes a large application.

FIGURE 2-13 Minimal Documentation

(COVER LETTER FORMAT)

TO:

FROM:

SUBJECT: (APPLICATION TITLE)

(Brief description of the application.)

(Brief Description of the management objectives.)

(Give names of concerned parties and organizations.)

ATT: (List attachments to the extend they exist. There should be attachments for the following three documents as a minimum.)

Technical Feasibility Study
Cost/Benefits Analysis
Sensitivity Analysis (may be merged into the Cost /Benefits Analysis)

FIGURE 2-14 Full Documentation

(COVER LETTER FORMAT)

TO:

FROM:

SUBJECT: DOCUMENTATION ON
(APPLICATION LONG TITLE & ABBREVIATION)

SUMMARY: (BRIEF DESCRIPTION OF APPLICATION)

(DESCRIPTION OF MANAGEMENT OBJECTIVES)

(STATE THE AUTHORITY/APPROVAL FOR
DEVELOPING THIS APPLICATION)

FIGURE 2-14 (continued)

TECHNICAL FEASIBILITY STUDY

(Describe the study in one paragraph to one page.
Reference the study by giving its name and attachment/appendix letter number.)

COST/BENEFIT ANALYSIS

(Reference this study document by its title and number in the attachment to this letter.)

Analysis (Describe the general analysis method followed, state the names of key contributors and major organizations involved. Note objections raised during the analysis, and explain how they were answered and why. Reference attachment and pertinent page numbers in the attachment.)

Summary (Provide a one-or-two paragraph summary of the C/B Analysis.)

Application Cost

(Give highlights of costs and reference pages in the attachment that provide supporting detail.)

Benefits Analysis

(Give highlights of benefits and reference pages in the attachment that provide supporting detail.)

SENSITIVITY ANALYSIS

(Reference this study document by its title and number in the attachment to this letter.)

Costs (Identify the major cost factors and the possibilities of their change in value. One or two paragraphs is needed.)

Benefits (Identify major benefit factor and the possibilities of their change in value. One or two paragraphs is needed.)

Assumptions (State principal assumptions made in performing this sensitivity analysis. One or two paragraphs is needed.)

## D. SUMMARY

Evaluating alternative solutions is an essential step in successfully implementing a computer application. The evaluation process eliminates poor solutions before spending large amounts of money and time. In addition, the evaluation process points out the most desirable solutions at the beginning of the manager's planning process, so that the best overall solution may be chosen. Documenting the manager's needs is useful during the evaluation process. The reason is that overly stringent time schedules for performing the implementation or for processing data, along with skimpy funding and special equipment capabilities and limitations, may be identified and taken into consideration before plans have been set. Despite the apparent formality and the technical computer knowledge involved, the formats presented are generally easily used by supervisors and managers who are not EDP-oriented.

# 3

# Analyzing requirements

## A. INTRODUCTION

After the management problem has been stated in the form of objectives and general definitions, it must be further expanded. In the expanded statement, called a Requirements Analysis, objectives and definitions are given in precise terms, and transformed into a statement of the functional computer processes.

This process can be complicated, as well as replete with technical terms and concepts that discourage many competent non-ADP managers. However, this process is too important to be left without continuing management input. Poor management advice can easily double expected cost and result in a mediocre application. Guidance is needed from the responsible manager, who has an understanding of the operating environment and the course of development and implementation of the proposed application. The Requirements Statement should include all items which the manager thinks important. Since some of the computer processes and jargon may be unfamiliar, their development in the Requirements

Statement will depend on the computer expert's assistance. As a minimum, the manager should outline preferences on how computer terminals and output reports are to be used, what computer services are expected, and how large the computer's job will be. The entire Requirements Analysis process may be simplified and largely eliminated if the planned application is small or straight forward, or if the necessary software can be purchased, leased, or adopted from existing software.

This chapter is divided into several sections. The first section defines the circumstances in which a formal Requirements Statement is needed. The succeeding sections contain a description of the analysis process, the Functional Requirements statement, and related manual processing. The explanation is intended to give you a general understanding of the process necessary, and to "walk" you through the process in a fashion that will help you put your needs into a form that will guide computer experts in preparing a quick and satisfactory solution.

## B. APPLICATION CHARACTERISTICS

Almost every proposed computer application needs a Functional Requirements Analysis to define the development process and specify expected results. The analysis itself must reflect the characteristics of the proposed application, including its scope, time constraints, processing logic, and related manual processing and end products. The definition process is often more difficult in practice than anticipated. As a result, the manager's initial problem definition is often viewed by the DP expert as neither firm nor definitive.

### 1. The Analysis Process

Analyzing a proposed computer application may be performed in steps and has various limitations in performance, reflecting the personalities, positions, and capabilities of the manager, the DP expert, and their staff. Both manager and DP expert expect an application that will work and be operational within a reasonable time period and within a reasonable budget. However, as the analysis task develops, typical factors in the initial definition may change (the original time schedule for planning the application, dates for performing the implementation, length of time for processing, and scope of data included). Judgment of what is reasonable is subjective and likely to change during this time.

The approach to follow must be a totally cooperative effort. The first step is largely and logically taken by the manager, who must state in writing the definition of the objectives. This material may be prepared by the manager or with a staff.

The second step consists of a discussion or series of discussions between the manager and the DP expert to insure a mutual understanding of the desired DP application needs. The computer expert must start by taking this initial definition and transforming it into corresponding functional computer processes, using charts, graphic analysis, and other clarifying techniques. Given a careful explanation of this analysis, the manager will normally gain additional insight into the problem so that it can be revised and better defined. If the manager cannot communicate easily with the DP expert, the lack of understanding will be apparent quickly, so it can be corrected. If the application is unique to the DP expert, the written documentation provides the expert with a basis for discussing the problem with technical specialists. This approach leads to good workable solutions and tends to eliminate embarrassing and expensive failures. In a simple system in which there is great talent and insight on the part of both manager and DP expert, several iterations of definition and redefinition are likely. In complex applications, the redefinition process and the improvements of the requirements definition frequently take place in small pieces over a long period of time.

This process of improving the requirements definition is often treated as tiresome and unimportant. Actually it is very important, since it eliminates costly major errors in the entire project--from the design stage, through implementation, and into actual regular operation. At the same time, it insures that the manger is fully aware of progress, the dollar cost, and time delay of problems. This process of requirements definition is suitable, no matter what types of analysis methods the DP expert uses.

Although this process is understandable, its application is often more difficult than expected because of three situations:

a. the user-manager does not know exactly what is needed,

b. the manager knows what is wanted, but cannot make the DP expert understand, or
c. the application is unusual in the sense that its characteristics are outside the DP expert's background and understanding.

These three situations are not unusual. The manager should expect them to appear in some form. If requirements were very easily determined, they would have been defined long ago, and would not require any DP expertise to implement.

The requirements analysis process should emphasize flexibility, since improved definition of the initial management requirement, compromises between conflicting requirements, and revisions to meet needs of other corporate managers often occur during the process.

## 2. Application Scope

A planned computer application may be limited in scope to a modest improvement in an existing application, or it may be much more extensive. A major change in a simple application will require modest effort and cost. Major changes in a complex application may be as difficult and costly as programming an entirely new application from scratch. Scope is also a function of geography: for instance, an application dealing with sales records may encompass the Philadelphia area, the Southeastern Pennsylvania area, including southern New Jersey, the East Coast, or the continental United States. A sales analysis might also be limited in scope according to product: for example, rebuilt GM carburetors from the Los Angeles plant versus an analysis dealing with all rebuilt carburetors from that plant.

The scope of an application should be carefully and completely stated. If the scope might be enlarged or modified, the possibility of such change should be noted, so that the analysis process can reflect this need for flexibility.

## 3. Time Constraints

Every proposed computer application is subject to a variety of time constraints, including:

a. time (date) at which the application must be operational,
b. schedule and number of hours required on the computer system to test the planned application,

c. schedule and amount of computer analyst and programmer manhours needed to complete and implement the application,
d. date by which mangement approval must be received, if the project is to be performed,
e. time cycle to receive input,
f. time cycle necessary to perform processing, and
g. time cycle to be followed for satisfactory delivery of the end product or results.

**4. Processing Flow Logic**

An application may be characterized by its proposed processing logic. The simplest processing logic is a straight line flow from input through processing to output. However, processing logic is often more complicated. As complexity is introduced, the application becomes more powerful, as well as more prone to logical error and more difficult to modify in the future. As each complexity is added, the logic is gradually transformed from a simple straight line process to a labyrinth.

Typical processing includes editing of input, sequencing of data, comparison of input data and existing files, and formatting of output reports. Many other logical steps may be involved, as well as steps to collect totals, counts, and so on. Editing involves various steps to insure that the input data is correct, is appropriate and is organized correctly. For example, sales data from cash registers may be checked to insure that only valid department numbers, sales numbers, and stock numbers have been entered, so that errors will not be introduced in subsequent sales analysis processing. Editing of payroll often includes comparison of gross earnings amounts to maximum allowable. Editing of automobile parts orders will generally involve verifying that the part order numbers match against current valid parts numbers. Errors detected in the editing may be handled by completely rejecting the entire data input or by rejecting just the erroneous portion. At this point, reentry of the data and manual correction procedures are often involved.

In some instances, information is entered into the computer application system in a completely random sequence, such as deposits and withdrawals received by tellers in a bank. When files are designed for random access processing, this type of data input may be quite satisfactory. In some situations, input transaction data will be processed against master files that must be kept in numeric sequence, such as homeowners' mortgage loan records. In these situations, the input transaction data must be sorted into sequence to match the master file or the processing routine must be designed to accept random processing.

Input information is often compared to an existing master file. When the input data matches an existing record, the existing record is updated. If the input data concerns refrigerated railroad boxcars, then the inventory records on, say, unassigned cars, are reduced by the number and style of cars assigned to a shipper. If the input data concerns sales of term life insurance policies, then the amount of term life insurance sold during this period is increased by the amount of the transactions, and the amount of commission due the insurance agency is increased accordingly.

Advantages of straight line processing logic include ease of correction and modification, as well as simplicity in testing and auditing. Straight line processing logic is also easily understood and summarized for management personnel who desire only an overall familiarity or who do not have the time to study a complex application. Unfortunately, some applications are just not suited to straight line processing. However, in some of the more complex processing logic, portions can be organized for straight line processing. Whenever possible, use straight line processing.

## C. MANUAL PROCESSING

Planning for a computer application should always include planning for related manual processing. This planning is easily overlooked or given inadequate attention because of the appeal and complexity of the computer-oriented work, and because manual processing is not the major focus of a computer application. Manual processing may be the critical item in implementing a successful application, because the personnel involved may, and often do, control the actual machine processing. Therefore, it should be carefully planned, documented, and understood by the personnel involved. Manual processing may be involved at any step of the total data processing operation including:

a. input,
b. formatting,

c. error correction,
d. exceptions processing,
e. output production,
f. output formatting,
g. distribution,
h. storage of data, and
i. storage of printed reports.

Often a choice may be made between manual or automated processing for one or several steps in an application. Consider the following eight factors in making this choice:

a. processing volume,
b. variability in processing volume,
c. irregular occurrence of special processing,
d. unknown or unforeseen processing needs,
e. costs of personnel for processing,
f. availability of trained personnel,
g. equipment/techniques available, and
h. cost of equipment/techniques.

Processing exceptions is one of the most common manual processing steps in a computer application. If there are few exceptions, the costs and time for manual processing may be very reasonable compared to automation. Orders received for quantities in excess of normal production runs may be treated as an exception and require an elaborate automated procedure to schedule delivery of the order at intervals, or to split the order between several factories. Such exception processing can be handled simply by directly referring the item to the manufacturing vice president or other appropriate official.

Another common reason for utilizing manual processing is the lack of a satisfactory automated technique. For example, a decision based on a complex set of facts (locating a new manufacturing plant, restructuring corporate marketing plans, redesigning a complex major production line) is better suited to decision-making by an appropriate executive than by a computer program. When computer programs are used in these circumstances, the final decisions are invariably left to approval by an appropriate executive or group of executives.

When extensive manual procedures are involved (for certain retailing functions, insurance company operations, bank teller positions), the DP expert may share responsibility for analyzing requirements with office systems analysts, industrial engineers, or other appropriate personnel.

## D. DOCUMENTING THE ANALYSIS

The process of analyzing functional requirements generates pages of material of various types. The analysis itself is better understood and more likely to be complete if it is carefully recorded, as well as carefully performed. The results of the process commonly fit into a Functional Requirements Statement. In large complex applications, an Expanded Data Requirements Statement is also prepared. In all cases, clearly specify appropriate manual procedures.

### 1. The Functional Requirements Statement

The Functional Requirements Statement adds considerable depth to the previously prepared Project Request form, Feasibility Study, and Cost/Benefit Analysis. The DP expert's function normally prepares the Functional Requirements Statement, based on the manager's input. The more complex the application, the more likely that the statement will be prepared and reviewed in successive drafts. The statement should always be reviewed and approved by the user-manager to insure that assumptions are reasonable and that development schedules and estimated costs are realistic. If the computer application is small and straight forward, the Functional Requirements Statement may be unimportant and can be ignored, for example if the total task will take the DP expert less than two weeks. This document should be prepared as an independent, stand-alone document, which references the previously prepared Project Request, Feasibility Study, and Cost/Benefit Analysis.

An abbreviated form of this document is shown in Figure 3-1. However, some applications require more detail. An expanded version of the Functional Requirements Statement is shown in Figure 3-2. If a manager needs more depth in a specific application, one or more portions of this expanded version will be useful. If the expanded form is needed, an additional document, the Data Requirements Document, is undoubtedly also needed. That document is explained in Figure 3-3.

FIGURE 3-1 Functional Requirements Statement

I. ADMINISTRATIVE INFORMATION

A. IDENTIFICATION
1. Project Title/Name
2. Reference Number
3. Requesting Organization and Manager
4. DP Contact
5. Data Statement Prepared
6. Reference Documents

II. SUMMARY

A. PERFORMANCE OBJECTIVES (Results expected)

B. ENVIRONMENT (Type users, physical setting)

III. OVERVIEW

A. EXISTING METHODS AND PROCEDURES

B. PROPOSED METHODS AND PROCEDURES

C. IMPACTS

IV. TECHNICAL REQUIREMENTS

A. QUALITATIVE AND QUANTITATIVE RESULTS

B. INPUT/OUTPUT

C. EFFECTS OF FAILURE

V. OPERATING ENVIRONMENT

A. EQUIPMENT

B. SOFTWARE AND SOFTWARE CONTROL

C. OTHER RELATED COMPUTER APPLICATIONS

D. SECURITY AND PRIVACY

VI. DEVELOPMENT PLAN

A. DOCUMENTATION REQUIRED

B. RESPONSIBLE ORGANIZATIONS

FIGURE 3-2 Expanded Functional Requirements Statement

## I. ADMINISTRATIVE INFORMATION

A. IDENTIFICATION
1. Project Title/Name (include abbreviation, if any)
2. Contract or Reference Number
3. Requesting Organization and Manager
4. Principal DP Project Contact
5. Date Statement Prepared
6. Type of Requirement

B. REFERENCE DOCUMENTS
1. Identify project request authorizing this application.
2. Identify other pertinent references.

## II. SUMMARY

A. OBJECTIVES
1. Describe the general end objectives.
2. List performance objectives.
3. Summarize anticipated results.

B. ENVIRONMENT
1. Identify end users.
2. Describe expected physical environment.

## III. OVERVIEW

A. EXISTING METHODS AND PROCEDURES (complete if an improvement, upgrade, or for cost reduction).

B. PROPOSED METHODS AND PROCEDURES

C. IMPACT OF PROPOSED METHODS AND PROCEDURES
1. Equipment
2. Software
3. Organization
4. Operational
5. Developmental
6. Cost and Resources Considerations
7. Alternative Applications Software

FIGURE 3-2 (continued)

IV. TECHNICAL REQUIREMENTS

A. PERFORMANCE REQUIREMENTS (Data characteristics, accuracy and validity, timeliness, qualitative and quantitative results)

B. INPUTS/OUTPUTS (Sources, types)

C. EFFECTS OF FAILURE (Loss of business, production line stopped)

V. OPERATING ENVIRONMENT

A. EQUIPMENT

B. SOFTWARE

C. RELATIONSHIP TO OTHER COMPUTER APPLICATIONS

D. SECURITY AND PRIVACY REQUIRED

E. SOFTWARE CONTROLS NEEDED

VI. DEVELOPMENT PLAN

A. DOCUMENTATION REQUIRED

B. RESPONSIBLE ORGANIZATIONS

FIGURE 3-3 Data Requirements Document

I. ADMINISTRATIVE INFORMATION

1. Project Title/Name
2. Contact or Reference Number
3. Requesting Organization and Manager
4. Principal DP Project Contact
5. Date of Preparation
6. Pertinent References

II. DATA DEFINITION

1. Input (Reference/Processed/Parameters)
2. Internally Generated (Use)
3. Output (Regular/Exceptions/Parameters)

III. DATA COLLECTION/DISTRIBUTION

1. Input Source and Responsibility
2. Input Media and Device
3. Input Procedures
4. Update and Processing Frequency
5. Output Media and Device
6. Recipients

The Functional Requirements Statement starts with an Administrative Information section, which is largely a cross reference to the previously prepared documents. Next the Summary section repeats and improves previous explanations of the expected results and describes the proposed environment. For example, the application will be used by skilled technicians, accounting clerks, part-time sales clerks, managers, and so on. The application will use keyboard devices on a receiving platform, keyboards and display screens in an office, printers in a warehouse, or the like. Anticipate each physical rearrangement and air conditioning and power change.

The Overview section summarizes present and proposed methods and procedures. The comparison between the present and proposed methods leads to a discussion of the impact of the proposed application: what new or changed equipment will be needed, what new instruction manuals and manual procedures will be needed, what reassignment and retraining of personnel is expected, and what costs will be increased or changed?

The Technical Requirements section reflects the data processing expert's input. The characteristics of the data should be explained, such as quantity, type, accuracy. Thus, the data may be all alphabetic vs. all numeric, it may involve thousands of 50-digit inventory records vs. hundreds of 300-character merchandise orders, or it may require validation against existing files, such as authorizing check payments against unpaid purchase orders. Timeliness and flexibility of the application should be described: it may be necessary to have all input data on sales received by 6:00 P.M. Friday, so that computer processing may be completed with reports available Monday morning at 9:00 A.M. Such time requirements for processing could be a management problem, if data processing is performed in New York, while the sales data includes Los Angeles and other West Coast cities (6:00 P.M. West Coast store closings are actually occurring at 9:00 P.M. Eastern time). Explain inputs and outputs.

If special output forms are needed, such as prenumbered paycheck stock, no carbon or spot carbon multipart forms, they may have a two-month design and order cycle, plus a two-month delivery cycle, plus substantial costs. If input is in the form of documents, these documents may be either handwritten or typed, requiring the time and expense to enter it into a DP system. Typed documents are not always correctly typed. If optical scanning is intended, certain type styles, like the IBM type ball (Printing and Publication #173), may be suitable, but not used by many input locations who do not know what type ball is needed.

The technical approach to use in meeting an application should reflect an understanding of the consequences if the application fails, and what is meant by the term "failure." In some instances a delay in processing of several hours may be of no consequence, so that rerunning the application is allowable (a weekly inventory report of standard building products in a home building supplies store). In other cases, a very short delay is considered intolerable (failure of a credit verification system or a bank securities transaction system). If failure has serious consequences, backup computer equipment and manual procedures may be required. Some failure conditions, such as electrical power aberrations, are poorly understood by many computer centers and may reappear.

The Operating Environment section is used to describe what equipment and software is expected to be available to support this proposed application. It is also used to describe other computer applications to which the proposed application relates, and security and privacy considerations that may be present. In some situations, the proposed application requires that a specific computer system be available with a certain number and type of disks, tapes, and other peripherals. If the peripheral units are changed or unavailable because of another use, it may be impossible to run the proposed application. If another computer system must be used, that other system may not have the necessary peripherals. Even if a computer system has the right combination of units to run an application, it may not have the internal instructions (systems software) to support the proposed application as designed. Specify the computer system and the minimum number of peripheral units and software needed.

If the proposed application uses a data file that has been processed and prepared by or for another application, note this fact. Personnel responsible for the other application should be aware that a change in their data file could affect this proposed application. In using another data file the proposed application could interfere with the unrestricted access of the original users, which could be a problem if timeliness is critical to that application.

Certain computer applications deal with information that must be protected from unauthorized users. As a matter of company policy, financial records are not for public information. Individual medical records are considered private, as a matter of law. Whenever company policy, law, or customer needs require controlling the accuracy of records or processing, state these requirements.

The last major section of the Functional Requirements Statement is the Development Plan. A time schedule, in the form of a chart or a list of milestones and completion dates, is needed, along with estimates of costs involved. In addition, explain what documentation will be needed at the completion of the application, such as a user manual. Identify other organizations concerned with developing this application and give the name and telephone number of the person to contact.

## 2. The Expanded Functional Requirements Statement

If a proposed application is complex or has some special problems, more detail may be desired in the

Functional Requirements Statement. One or more portions of the expanded statement (Figure 3-2) may be used to develop this additional information, explained in the following paragraphs.

Administrative Information in a large complex application may be expanded to include specific reference to individuals by title, telephone number, and office. The complexity of the application and its relation to others makes it worthwhile to indicate whether the application is a new development, a revision, or a modification. Documents related to the application should be identified with title, date, author, reference number, and physical location, such as a company library, data processing department file, or similar.

The Summary section of the expanded statement contains considerably more information than needed for the less complicated application. State end objectives, such as completion date, security, training needed, and specific benefits. Also state performance objectives, such as quantity of data, processing cycle allowed, output formats and distribution, operation dates, and budget. Spell out anticipated results for complex applications: gives new capability in terms of reports and their distribution; upgrades capability, such as graphs and charts in color; eliminates deficiencies, such as verification and editing of terminal input online; achieves timeliness, such as a reduction in processing time from one day to two hours for an important batch processing application. Also, describe the type of work and anticipated physical environment: professional, clerical, or technical work; new floor plans, rebuilding, air conditioning, power lines.

The Overview section discusses present and proposed methods and impact. If the proposed application is an upgrade or improvement, give an explanation regarding both the present and the proposed application. The explanation should discuss the organization involved, employees, each position's responsibilities, equipment, location of employees and equipment, processing cycle, costs, deficiencies, and present inputs and outputs. Include a simplified logical processing chart.

The impact of the proposed application should be discussed in seven areas:

a. Equipment presently installed may require change, or modification and relocation. New equipment may be required. Offices and buildings may require rewiring, air conditioning, and other physical alterations.

b. Existing computer software may be indispensible in running the new application. If this application depends on files, records, or outputs from other software, explain these needs.

c. Organizational impact is frequently important. Changes in the number of employees, types of skills, and skill levels required may necessitate training. Specify if training is needed, so that cost and scheduling may be planned.

d. A number of operation impacts may occur. Describe changes involved, such as user operating procedures, relationships between the data processing center and users, data inputs (types, sources, handling procedures, frequency, quantity, time schedules, active retention period, storage and retrieval), DP center procedures and processing cycles, application failure consequences, and recovery procedure.

e. Describe development impact, such as requirements for the user to prepare sample data, rearrange work station, or temporarily reassign personnel. Explain computer processing services necessary to develop and test the application, such as computer size, memory size, number of disks and tapes, systems software, schedule of test time.

f. Explain cost and availability of resource factors

--Availability of suitable terminals or printers (field sales representatives already have terminals which can be used for this new application, such as insurance sales representatives who have terminals to analyze potential customers' insurance coverage and can use the same terminals to record sales applications).

--Availability of special expertise (company data communications expert can estimate costs for use of dial-up inquiry on inventory during day versus single call in evening after 6:00 P.M.).

--Availability of information from an existing computer application (Mailings to customers can be developed from presently available billing addresses in sales records, and from standard sales order entry file). Cost quotation system for new machinery may be developed by using manufacturing parts cost analysis file, new parts estimates, and standard product cost formulas, rather than by estimating the entire product.

--Availability of existing computer software (such as using Informatics Corporation's MARK IV* software system to prepare certain reports rather than spend time and effort in company programming).

g. Describe known alternative applications software. List major available software packages. If there are none, explain. If other software is not suitable, explain why not. If software is only available from an outside ADP vendor, explain why this alternative should or should not be considered. Rate all known software packages. Compare the cost of installation, continuing cost, maintenance problems, computer limitation, documentation shortcomings, time to verify and install, and so on.

The Technical Requirements section is used to describe qualitative and quantitative features required of the proposed computer application (must be able to process 200 transactions per minute against a master file, must be capable of processing existing 12-digit accounting codes).

Subsection A explains Performance Requirements. Required details are organized into four subsections, including data characteristics, data accuracy and validity required, time factors, and application flexibility. At a minimum, list each and every data element, giving its name and definition, including such factors as number of characters, and type characters (alpha/alphanumeric/numeric only). Indicate the possibility of adding or revising the list of data elements, and the circumstances under which such changes are likely.

The data accuracy required may be implied by the data: hospital pharmacy records or controlled drugs must identify types, quantities, and specific use to meet legal requirements. Calculations of daily interest earned typically will be to the nearest cent. Calculation of interest expense for future capital investments may be rounded to the nearest larger dollar. Inventory information to be transmitted to corporate accounting will not include work-in-process, since this inventory is very small.

Explain data validity required: weekly salaries shall not exceed $1,000 gross each, employees with savings allotments to the company's matching funds plan may not have allotments in excess of 15 percent of gross salary nor less than $25, input data on wholesale orders must have both a valid sales number and a valid customer code.

Frequently the time factors involved are critical: response time for online transactions shall not exceed ten seconds 95 percent of the time and shall never exceed twenty seconds. Manufacturing schedules will be completely updated each night, starting at 6:00 P.M., and shall be available by 8:00 A.M. at various distribution centers.

Application flexibility is often a major concern. Describe the necessary capability for the application to be modified: must accept twelve-digit part numbers instead of existing ten-digit; be operational on DEC* equipment, rather than the existing IBM* equipment; be suitable for implementation on WANG* equipment, as well as the present UNIVAC* processor, be able to accept input data from U.S. Census Bureau computer tapes or from an industry or trade association data file. (*Denotes Trademark names.)

Subsection B itemizes impact on input/output. Itemize the data impact including an example of each. Specify the medium (tapes, removable digital cassette from terminals). Specify the format of each input and acceptable variations, give range of values on each item of data, give quantities anticipated, and so on. List the outputs, including an example of each hardcopy report, CRT screen display, graphic output, and data transmission. Explain formats, accuracy involved, frequency of output, and the like.

Subsection C explains the effects of failure. Describe the events that would be considered a failure of the computer application: delay in on-line processing of thirty seconds compared to the normal maximum of ten seconds, a delay in batch processing of more than one hour, a failure of a CRT screen in the production control office that occurs between 6:00 A.M. and 9:00 A.M. during the week, a failure of a CRT screen in the production control office that lasts more than one hour, incorrect processing that results in the loss of a sales order. Describe the cost and losses that result from a computer failure: go out of business if accounts receivable records are lost, lose $50,000 in airline ticket sales if terminals fail for five minutes, suffer loss of profit of $10,000 if real time response for stock broker slows down to thirty seconds, and so forth.

Explain backup plans: extra copies of files will be maintained on another computer system, on a tape, in hard paper copies of order documents, shipping documents, manufacturing job tickets, and the like.

Explain fallback plans: another automated or manual system will be used to perform the computer application or critical parts of the application, such as a duplicate system at another location, a smaller system in a branch office, a service bureau, or a temporary manual file.

Explain recovery and restart plans. Specify how the computer application can be restarted, if a failure does occur: using checkpoint/restart routines, taking periodic data dumps of a computer program, maintaining a protected file of data that can be copied and used to restart.

Section V describes the Operating Environment. It consists of five subsections: Equipment, Software, Relationship to other Computer Applications, Security and Privacy Required, and Software Controls needed.

Identify support equipment. State major components required: for instance, specify that four online IBM 3350 disks are needed, since available disks may be monopolized by other customers when your application requires them. Include information on the anticipated central processing unit, high speed internal storage, external storage devices, both online and offline. Describe input/output devices of all types, including microfilm processors, optical character readers (OCR), tapes and disks, including capacity and speed when appropriate. Describe required data communications/front end processors.

If this computer application depends upon a specific software operating system or proprietary software, name the software, identifying the particular version/revision. If necessary changes are expected to be made in the software, note the nature and planned date of these changes. If these changes do not take place, the proposed application may not run on the computer.

If this computer application depends upon data provided by another computer application, state this fact. Identify use of other software to the personnel controlling changes in the other software, so that no change is made which would make it impossible to run your application.

Describe state, federal, or company requirements for security and privacy of data: credit reference files, loan history records, medical data. If there are no special security or privacy needs state the fact.

Changes in software often have operational controls imposed. Describe such controls and sources. If no controls are known, indicate the extent to which controls are needed.

Section VI describes how the application will be developed. Describe the general plan for development and implementation. Include a list of documentation that should be produced, including who is responsible for producing it. Specify time schedules and milestones; describe all necessary approvals; establish a distribution list for documentation. Describe other involved organizations, units, branches, contractors, indicating the responsible person to contact in that organization.

## 3. The Data Requirements Document

This document is a technical statement, shown in Figure 3-3, which describes in detail the data needed for the application, and how and where the data will be collected. Although prepared by the DP expert, it should be reviewed and approved by the user-manager. Data Requirements must be reasonable and realistic; only the user-manager is in a position to judge and advise changes.

The Data Requirements Document is readily organized into three sections. The importance of each subsection depends upon the characteristics of the specific application.

The Administrative Information section identifies the document and links it to other documentation for this application, with name of project, reference numbers, identification of the requesting organization manager and of the DP contact, dates, and references.

The Data Definition section describes the data based on its appearance as input or as output. Identify as input an item of data, such as an invoice number. Then explain its use as a reference or for processing. As a reference item, this data element would have to appear and would have to be allowable, or the sales could not be processed.

Explain procedures for manually assembling input documents, for keypunching or typing inputs, and for storing input documents. Describe the frequency of updating and processing, especially if they are irregular or are tied to an outside event, such as calendar date, as would sales of Christmas trees or women's fashions for Easter. In other instances, weather conditions may be the controlling factor, as in the case of winter heating oil sales and ski trips. In the same fashion, explain output media and devices, as well as the number, location, and types of users.

In the final section, describe the processes of data collection and distribution. Explain the input source (organization/group) and its responsibility (sales representative's input, sales data, sales order clerk's, correct product and customer codes). If input data is received over data communication wires attached to a specific type of terminal, explain. Note other special inputs. For example, computer tapes may be received from large customers. Or the number on the invoice might be restricted to, say, a six-digit number prefaced by the letters D or E. Any other invoice number would be recognized as improper, and the transaction would be rejected. If the data element were a rate per $1,000 of insurance, this rate would be multiplied by the amount sold to verify the total sales dollars. In some instances, the data element will be internally generated, such as a sequential sales number or a sales number that incorporates the transaction date. Output data may include such items as discounts allowed based on quantity, size of sales, or cumulative sales. If discounts are involved, the amounts, percentages, and products may be restricted to specific values.

## E. SUMMARY

After defining a general approach for the proposed computer application, define the application. Small applications require a minimum of paperwork. Larger and critical applications require more specific definition and paperwork. In large applications at least, the requirements analysis process appears to be a sizable task and this often induces managers and computer experts to do only a minimum job. In practice, the unexpected costs and delays that are encountered because of an inadequate requirements analysis are likely to cost more than preparing a proper analysis. The basic formats used for requirements analysis are described in detail in this chapter and may be used as a guide for the manager's proposed application.

# 4

# Implementing the application

## A. INTRODUCTION

After the proposed application has been defined and documented, decide how it will be implemented. Anticipated costs and promised completion dates may differ significantly among the four major approaches:

1. Have the computer application programmed and run at the inhouse computer center.
2. Purchase or lease packaged programs (software) for use at the computer center.
3. Contract for custom computer applications programming for software to be run at the computer center.
4. Contract with a service bureau or a time-share vendor to provide the applications software and the computer equipment.

This chapter describes these choices and explains the principal factors you must consider when selecting an alternative.

## B. INHOUSE DATA PROCESSING

The first organization to contact in reviewing implementation alternatives is usually the inhouse data center. This practice helps to insure that the corporation's inhouse facilities are used to the maximum prior to expending funds for outside services. Often, the corporate data center will be selected to develop and improve a data processing application, with only a perfunctory consideration of the advantages of using an outside service bureau or buying packaged software or services from a vendor. After comparing inhouse and outside costs and services, the inhouse data center is frequently selected, because its equipment, personnel, software, and methods of operation are known.

### 1. Equipment Availability

The inhouse center's personnel are often able to assist a user-manager in understanding general DP technology by demonstrating working examples of different speed, type, and style printers, CRTs, and typewriter-style terminals.

An inhouse function may reassign existing computer terminals or use them part-time to support initial computer programming or to enter sample input data. Existing central processing equipment may have unused capacity. However, this capacity may be available only on an irregular schedule or in varying amounts, so that it cannot be relied upon to support the development of a new application.

The inhouse DP center may not have the required specialized equipment, such as a high-speed printer or computer-output-microfilm (COM). If equipment is not available now, the manager must find out if it will be available in the future or the proposed application cannot be operated at the center. In some instances, limited inhouse equipment availability will leave the manager with no choice but to have the application developed and operated at a service bureau or by a time-share vendor.

### 2. Software Availability

Existing general purpose software may be used to accept sample input data, perform limited processing, and provide simple, but useful, output reports. The opportunity to develop quickly a basic version of the projected application is a great advantage, since it shows whether assumptions are realistic and practical. For instance, input data will be received on a timely basis via mail, errors can be easily and quickly corrected, the instructions provided for coding input data are understood by the users in field locations. If any of these assumptions are unrealistic, some problems will appear almost immediately, so that the manager and the DP expert can identify them and revise their approach.

There are many combinations of DP work that can be supported by an inhouse center. If the center specializes in mathematical modeling, it might not have the software to support general business applications. When specialized software is not available at the center or is not expected to be installed, find out if the center will install other software to support the proposed application and determine who will pay for such software. In this instance, a general software package from an outside vendor might be an immediate cost-effective solution. The software needed for the proposed application could then be reduced to a very simple computer routine or to a minor modification of the packaged software. The time and cost savings are often substantial. If none of these alternatives are possible, consider contracting with a service bureau or a time-share vendor.

### 3. Contracting for Software Development

The data center may be limited in the number of qualified programmers who can be assigned to develop applications software. Under these circumstances, the data center must decide whether contracting with an outside computer programming service is a reasonable and timely alternative to in-house programming. In some instances the data center may have already established close working arrangements with one or more qualified software firms, and skilled assistance is readily available. In these circumstances, the data center may request estimates from a programming contractor to compare with inhouse development time and costs or with software package implementation time and costs.

### 4. Policy and Politics

The inhouse computer center accepts a degree of responsibility for the success of an application it programs and operates. If the inhouse center personnel advise the manager to obtain support services from a vendor, problems that arise could reflect on the competence of the inhouse center.

Unlike an outside vendor, the inhouse center manager and personnel are subject to pressure by the user-manager. An outside organization defines its responsibility in a contract, which may or may not have provisions that limit its responsibility. If the user-manager's application is unsuccessful, the user-manager may be reprimanded or dismissed, while the outside vendor is relatively unaffected.

Use of an inhouse data center may be advantageous when the user-manager or the user staff have working relationships with them: that is, they have an existing application at the computer center, or they have existing management or working level contacts. If a cooperative attitude already exists, it promotes timely action by both parties.

Applications which involve sensitive data, such as medical records, company profit margin analyses, prospective land purchases, estimates of underground oil or mineral reserves, are normally considered much more secure if they are developed and performed by the company data center rather than an outside vendor. Critical applications are often restricted to development and/or operation by the company data center on the premise that a high priority can be established and maintained more easily than if dealing with a vendor.

### 5. Planning and Scheduling

Inhouse DP personnel often have a better understanding of the user-manager's knowledge of DP technology and requirements for service than a vendor. As a result, the inhouse center may be more flexible in planning and scheduling to meet the manager's needs. The center may also be more cooperative in revising processing schedules, if a crisis should arise.

## C. PACKAGED SOFTWARE

In recent years, the similarity of computer applications between companies has become obvious. At the same time, the costs of developing an application have increased and skilled programmers have become more difficult to hire and retain. The financial risks of implementing new applications may also be significant. As a result, a large market has developed for packaged software.

Packaged software has become an attractive alternative to reprogramming, as the trend toward distributed processing has resulted in the installation of small computer systems throughout company headquarters and field offices. These smaller computer systems may or may not be compatible with large existing computer applications and equipment. Current applications can rarely be transferred between computer equipment without some software changes. These changes require programming staff support, and when incompatible equipment is involved, the present staff may lack hands-on experience.

Corporate accounting, payroll, and personnel systems were typically among the first computer applications in many companies, so they frequently have the most limited design and require the most reprogramming when the manager must distribute the application.

New computer systems provide highly desirable features that can only be taken advantage of by using the new systems software. When new equipment is installed at headquarters or field offices, existing applications programs must be modified to fit into the new software and to utilize its features.

An alternative to performing major design or reprogramming is to use packaged software. An appropriate software package can be used in part or total to reduce or eliminate programming time and expense. The manager should be aware that packaged software is widely available and may be a better choice than reprogramming an application.

## 1. Packaged Software Features

There are many software packages currently available from vendors or service bureaus. Any one type of software package may be implemented in a variety of ways. Figure 4-1 shows some features of available software packages, listed according to common organizational functions. Software features may include items such as account balances and totals for a large number of accounts, and summary and detailed records for accounts receivable and accounts payable. The specific features provided in one package are often performed differently in another similar software package. Some software packages provide additional features to foster easy use, including tables to enter identification names and codes, as well as optional capabilities that may be triggered by the user. If a package appears to provide a desired feature, the actual process performed should be evaluated against the requirements described in the completed Feasibility Study and other documentation.

FIGURE 4-1 Software Package Features Classified by Functions

| Software Package Feature | Functions 1 .1 | .2 | .3 | .4 | .5 | .6 | 2 | 3 | 4 | 5 | 6 | 7 | 8 |
|---|---|---|---|---|---|---|---|---|---|---|---|---|---|
| Account Balances | • | • | • | • | • | | • | | | | | • | |
| Accounting System | • | • | • | • | | | | | • | | | • | |
| Accounts Payable (On-line) | • | | | | | | | | | | | | |
| Accounts Receivable | | • | | | | | | | | | | | |
| Auditing, Internal | • | • | • | • | • | | • | | | | | | |
| Automatic Vacation Sick Pay Accruals | | | | | • | • | | | | | | | |
| Balance Sheets Projections | | | • | • | | | | • | | | | | |
| Bill of Material | | | | | | | | • | • | • | • | | |
| Billing | | • | • | | | | | • | | | | • | |
| Budget & Planning | | | • | • | | | • | • | • | • | • | • | |
| Bus Acctg & Mgmt System | | | • | • | | | • | • | • | • | • | | • |
| Bus Forecasting | | | • | | | | | • | | | • | • | |
| Capacity Planning | | | | | | | | • | | • | | | |
| Capital Budgeting | | | • | | | | | • | | • | | | |
| Cash Availability Flow | • | • | • | | | | • | • | | | | • | |
| Commercial Cooling & Heating Load | | | | | | | | | • | | | | • |
| Contract Status | | | | | | | | • | | | | • | |
| Cost Acctg | • | • | • | • | | | | | • | • | | | |

Functions: 1 = Accts, .1 = Accts Payable, .2 = Accts Receivable, .3 = Gen Accts, .4 = Gen Ledger, .5 = Payroll, .6 = Personnel, 2 = Finance & Insurance, 3 = Forecasting & Estimating, 4 = Inf Retrieval, 5 = Manufacturing, 6 = Purchasing, 7 = Sales & Marketing, 8 = All Others

FIGURE 4-1 (continued)

| Software Package Feature | Functions 1 .1 | .2 | .3 | .4 | .5 | .6 | 2 | 3 | 4 | 5 | 6 | 7 | 8 |
|---|---|---|---|---|---|---|---|---|---|---|---|---|---|
| Cost Control Estimating Gen/Mgmt Planning | | | • | | | | • | • | • | • | • | • | • |
| Customer Order Control/ Processing | | | | | | | | | | • | | • | |
| Data Base Control/Maintenance/Planning | | | | | | | | | • | | | | • |
| Data Collection System | | | | | | | | | • | | | | • |
| Data Control Security | | | | | | | | | • | | | | • |
| Depreciation | | | | • | | | | | • | • | | | • |
| Diagnostic History (Medical) | | | | | | | | | • | | | | • |
| Discount Calculation | | • | | | | | • | • | | | | • | |
| Dispatching (Priority) | | | | | | | | | | • | • | • | |
| Distributed Data Processing | • | • | | | | | • | | | • | • | • | • |
| Distribution Acctg/Req Planning | • | • | • | • | • | | • | • | | • | • | • | |
| Engineering Bill of Materials/ Data Control Design/Production/Production Control | | | | | | | | • | | • | • | | • |
| Equipment Mgmt | | | • | | | | | • | | | | | • |
| Fault Current Analysis | | | | | | | | • | | | | | • |
| File Maintenance | | | • | • | | | | • | • | | | | • |
| Financial Controls/Forecasting/Modeling/Mgmt Reports | | | | | | | • | • | • | | | | • |
| Forecasting (Demand/Historical) | | | | | | | • | • | • | | | | • |
| Forecasting and Analysis/Inv Analysis | | | | | | | • | • | • | • | • | | |
| Funds Transfer | | | | | | | • | • | | | | | |
| General Ledger Acctg/Accts Payable | • | | | • | | | | | | | | | |
| Insurance Billing (Medical) | | • | • | | | | | | | | | | • |

FIGURE 4-1 (continued)

| Software Package Feature | Functions 1 .1 | .2 | .3 | .4 | .5 | .6 | 2 | 3 | 4 | 5 | 6 | 7 | 8 |
|---|---|---|---|---|---|---|---|---|---|---|---|---|---|
| Inventory Acctg/Adjustment/ Control/Mgmt/Perpetual/ Planning/Physical/Records/ Status/Stores/Control | | | | | | | • | • | • | • | • | | |
| Job Costing/Forecasting/ Scheduling/Tracking/ Standards | | | | | | | | • | | • | | | |
| Labor Distribution/Per- formance Reports | | | | | • | • | | • | | • | | | |
| Ledger Reporting | | | | • | | | | | • | | | | |
| Mgmt Billing Info | | • | | | | | | • | | | | • | |
| Manufacturing Data Con- trol/Design/Engin- eering/Order Pro- cessing/Material & Stock Location/Stan- dards | | | | | | | | • | • | • | • | | |
| Material Control/Mgmt/ Online Mgmt/Planning/ Scheduling/Net Change Planning | | | | | | | | • | | • | • | | |
| Master Schedule/On Order | | | | | | | | | | • | • | | |
| Merger & Acquisition/ Analysis | | | | | | | • | | | | | | • |
| New Equip/Product Lease/ Purchase Analysis | | | | | | | • | | | | | • | • |
| Operating Plan Proformas | • | • | • | • | • | | • | • | | | | • | |
| Operational Scheduling & Loading/Routing | | | | | | | | • | | • | | • | |
| Order Entry/Costing/ Planning/Processing/ Release/Sales Analysis | | | | | | | | | • | • | • | • | |
| Parts Analysis | | | | | | | | | • | • | • | | |
| Patient Billing (Medical) | | • | | | | | | | | | | | • |
| Performance Reporting | | | | | | | | • | • | • | • | • | |
| Personnel | | | | | • | • | | • | • | | | | |
| Plotting Software | | | | | | | | | | | | | • |
| Processing & Routing | | | | | | | | | | | | • | |

FIGURE 4-1 (continued)

| | Functions<br>1 | | | | | | | | | | | | |
|---|---|---|---|---|---|---|---|---|---|---|---|---|---|
| Software Package Feature | .1 | .2 | .3 | .4 | .5 | .6 | 2 | 3 | 4 | 5 | 6 | 7 | 8 |
| Procurement Management System | | | | | | | | | | | • | | |
| Production Control Cost/Eng Data/Planning/Scheduling | | | • | | | | | • | | • | | | |
| Project Control/Cost/Info Mgmt | | | | | | | | • | • | • | | | |
| Purchase Order Control/ Mgmt/Processing/ Tracking | | | | | | | | | • | | • | | |
| Purchasing/Receiving (Dock to Stock) | | | | | | | | | • | • | • | | |
| Receivables | | • | | | | | | | • | | • | | |
| Report System English language inquiry) | | | | | | | | | | | | | • |
| Requirements Generation/ Pegging/Planning Simulation | | | | | | | | • | • | | | | |
| Resource Capacity Planning | | | | | | | | • | | • | | | |
| Retrieval (Ad Hoc/Records) | | | | | | | | | • | | | | • |
| Routing | | | | | | | | • | | | | • | |
| Sales Analysis/By Revenue Class/Forecasting/Trends | | | | | | | | • | | | | • | |
| Sales Order Entry/ Processing | | | | | | | | | | | | • | |
| Sales Projection & Requirements Scheduling | | | | | | | | | | | | • | |
| Shop Calendar | | | | | | | | | | • | | | |
| Shop Floor Control/Processing/Reporting | | | | | | | | | • | • | | | |
| Shop Order Control/Reporting | | | | | | | | | • | • | | | |
| Standard Costing/Job Order Costing/Product Costing | | | • | | | | | | | | | | |
| Stock Status & Order Entry | | | | | | | | | | | • | • | |
| Stock & Bond Record Processing | | | | | | | • | | | | | | • |
| Stock Market Quotation | | | | | | | • | | | | | | • |

FIGURE 4-1 (continued)

| Software Package Feature | Functions 1 .1 | .2 | .3 | .4 | .5 | .6 | 2 | 3 | 4 | 5 | 6 | 7 | 8 |
|---|---|---|---|---|---|---|---|---|---|---|---|---|---|
| Stores Control | | | | | | | | | | • | • | | |
| Tabular Data Analysis | | | | | | | | | | | | | • |
| Tax Calculations | | | • | • | • | | | | | | | | |
| Tax Table | | | • | • | • | | | | | | | | |
| Telephone Cost Analysis | | | • | • | | | | | • | | | | |
| Tool Inventory | | | | | | | | | | • | | | |
| Vendor Analysis & Purchasing/Performance Analysis | | | | | | | | | | • | | • | |
| Warehousing | | | | | | | | | | | | | • |
| Work in Process Control/ Costing/Monitoring/ Tracking | | | • | • | | | | | | • | | | |
| Work Center & Routing | | | | | | | | | | • | | | |
| Work Order Control/ Launching/Mgmt/ Preparation | | | | | | | | • | | • | | • | |

## 2. Evaluating Software Packages

Since there are hundreds of software vendors and many thousands of software packages available, the process of selection and evaluation is not trivial. With so many packages available, it is reasonable to believe that there may be appropriate software to meet the manager's needs. Savings as high as 80 percent of the original estimated cost have been cited in discussions with some apparently successful users. The manager and the DP expert should join with the inhouse computer center's operating personnel in evaluating packaged software, since these packages are frequently limited to operation only on a specific computer system which has certain minimum quantities or types of disks, memory, tapes, or other components.

Six major steps should be followed in evaluating packaged software for a planned application.

a. Determine exactly what is needed. Review existing documentation, including a Functional Requirements Statement and Cost/Benefit Analysis. For instance, special ways of establishing cost centers and charging between different levels of cost centers may be needed to meet the requirements of the application. If this requirement is not defined, a software package might be selected that does not provide the necessary features.

b. Prepare a list of the software requirements. State each and every specific capability required. If a personnel software package is involved, requirements might include providing space for twelve digits for a social security number (U.S./foreign), or providing for a foreign language field that can contain up to five language identifiers and ratings for speaking, reading, and writing ability. Also, list features which are desirable, but not obligatory: for example, it is desirable that a cost accounting package could be used to support up to twenty separate corporate cost centers.

c. Develop a list of potential software packages. A number of advisory services, special publications, trade magazines, or outside consultants may be used by the manager and/or the DP expert to assist in selecting the packaged software that is most likely to fill the manager's needs. This step is important, since it helps to prevent overlooking a possible software source. If there are actually only a few possible sources, the manager has an opportunity to reconsider the rigidity of the processing requirements, and consider cost savings that may be achieved by relaxing these requirements.

d. Obtain literature and review the most appropriate software packages. Vendor literature may state that specific requirements are met, although the literature may not describe the technique in any depth. The methods actually used could be significant in certain applications and may have to be evaluated. If a package appears to be a leading candidate for acquisition, the DP expert may arrange to test the package with sample data in the inhouse data center or otherwise to determine that the package works as needed.

e. Plan for implementation. Check the proposed software package to determine that it will operate in the company data center under normal conditions. Almost every software package requires some modifications. Is it reasonable to expect that necessary changes can be made in the data center to accomodate the package? How much assistance will the package vendor provide to implement the software? Will the package require major changes to the existing equipment and conflict with existing software? If so, what costs, time schedules and operational problems are likely to be involved? All changes needed should be identified and agreed to by the manager, the DP expert, and the data center operational manager.

f. Evaluate the vendor. If the software package is determined to be desirable and cost-effective, the manager and the DP expert should evaluate the vendor's support policies and financial durability. How does the vendor propose to support the package? Will the vendor supply updating documentation such as tapes and card decks, as improvements are made and inherent errors are detected and corrected? How long has the vendor been in business, and how long in the software package business? Does the vendor have sufficient financial resources to remain in business during the useful life of the package? Obviously, the best software package available at a low cost may become an expensive disaster, if it is not supported because the vendor is no longer in business.

## 3. Implementing Packaged Software

The ideal implementation of packaged software consists of mounting a reel of computer tape or entering a deck of punched cards into the computer system, along with actual data to produce the desired end product. Although this process rarely happens without difficulty, it never seems to happen if any operating conditions have changed in the initial installation of equipment. A detailed implementation plan is needed to insure that problems are minimized. Such a plan is often overlooked or given scant attention, since potential problems are considered unlikely by some package software representatives, and the manager and the DP expert may be overly optimistic and trusting. The manager must expect, and the DP expert insist, that adequate time and resources be planned for the implementation phase.

In the first step of successful implementation, carefully review all documentation supplied by the vendor. The DP expert largely performs this review, closely coordinated with the data center operations staff.

In the second step, plan the implementation process for a specific time and with a specific group of participants: the one reel of tape supplied by the vendor will be mounted by the operations crew at 10:00 A.M. Tuesday, under the immediate supervision of the operations chief and the DP expert. At this time, sample test data that has been prepared with the manager's advice will be available and will be processed through the software package.

The third step will focus on a review of the output results by the manager and the DP expert to identify any obvious errors, as well as desired changes. To assist in making this review, the manager and the DP expert should have prepared an outline of anticipated results, including samples of each expected result. The test data will include known erroneous data, so that exceptions processing can be verified.

The fourth step consists of making corrections and adjustments in the program until the software processing is acceptable. The last step involves obtaining signatures from all parties accepting the package for the corporation.

## D. CONTRACTING FOR APPLICATIONS SOFTWARE

Some computer applications have unique characteristics that are best satisfied by custom programming. This requires identifying an appropriate contractor and giving the contractor a copy of the requirements. The custom programming process involves locating qualified applications software suppliers, establishing the computer equipment to be used, defining the technical work, obtaining bids for service, placing an appropriate contract, and reviewing and accepting the software. The depth and extent of the manager's contracting effort reflects:

a. the probable costs and benefits of the programming work,
b. the skill and experience of the vendor selected, and
c. the skill and experience of the manager in dealing with this type of contract.

### 1. Custom Software Suppliers

Independent software vendors range in size from a one or two person local business to international organizations with thousands on their staff. One independent vendor may present unique experience and favorable costs. Another vendor may have performed many assignments programming similar applications. The vendor may be operating with relatively low cost part-time personnel and may be able to begin programming work earlier than the inhouse data center.

Potential vendors may be identified from a number of sources. The computer equipment vendor may have an expert programming staff available. If the manufacturer does not have staff available, they may refer a manager to known potential sources. An inhouse computer center may have used outside programming services in the past and be able to recommend potential vendors, or may be able to obtain such service and supervise it for the manager. Computer science faculty at nearby colleges and universities may be available to do programming for a fee. Vendors in the field may be located from computer industry trade journals and newspapers, reference books, classified pages of the telephone directory, professional associations, and through recommendations from other users. A small proposed application warrants only a limited effort in selecting a vendor.

## 2. Equipment Parameters

Selection of an outside programming vendor is often limited by the equipment to be used. If the manager expects to run the application on a very new, state-of-the-art equipment, it will be difficult to locate a firm with significant experience. If the equipment is both unique and specialized, such as ultra-high-speed disks or electronic memory, sophisticated phototypesetting units, or graphics output devices, effective use may be difficult to plan, because the equipment is not commonly understood. In other situations, an application must fit existing equipment, which limits the programmer in selecting an effective implementation method. If the computer hardware includes only a few disks, random selection and storage of data from large data bases may be slow compared to using the same make and model of computer equipment with many disks.

## 3. Contract Practices

Contracts are easy to sign, but may be costly if they have not been carefully reviewed prior to signature. The application to be programmed should be carefully defined, because errors in the original contract requirements will be corrected at the manager's expense. Later, minor changes to the contract requested by the user's or the manager's staff may cause additional expense. If these changes and modifications are not documented and have not been controlled as part of the contract, they may be used by a vendor to explain delays and increased costs.

If the manager supplies poor test data, the resulting application may appear to meet the contract requirements, but may not necessarily meet the manager's needs. Problems in the contracting process may result in substantial cost overruns, delays in completion, and unpleasant dealings with the software vendor that may affect future developments.

To insure timely performance and acceptable results, a penalty clause, may be desired by the manager especially with applications that appear to be expensive and take a long time to complete. This clause appears desirable, but may be ineffective in practice, if the contract does not also have clauses regarding changes in specifications and required delivery of documentation at intermediate steps. Large contracts should require intermediate results and delivery of documentation at the completion of each phase. If the intermediate results are available, the manager may choose to have delayed or unsatisfactory work completed by another vendor or by inhouse staff. If intermediate documentation and results are unavailable, the manager must resort to more drastic alternatives, such as accept the delay and/or increased costs, stop all work pending redo of the job by another vendor or by inhouse personnel, or sue for damages after the work is completed. Some of these choices will be impractical if, for instance, the software vendor goes bankrupt or the programmers actually performing the work resign. Always review contracts with legal counsel prior to signing.

## 4. The Request for Proposals

When software vendors are asked to quote on providing computer programming services, provide a Request for Proposals. This request may be divided into eight sections, including:

a. A standard format for identification of the vendor's technical and contract personnel. This should include such common items as names of the parties, corporate and local office addresses, and telephone numbers.

b. A specific format for the vendor to follow in submitting a proposal. This simplifies the task of comparing proposals.

c. A description of the computer equipment that will be used in running the completed application program. This insures that the software will fit the equipment.

d. Technical specifications to be met, including factors unique to computer programming. This includes style, type and format of computer software documentation to be supplied, which party prepares the test data, personnel to be assigned (including resumes), how the customer (manager) approves the test data and intermediate results, how the customer will be given an opportunity to review and modify draft documentation, how changes or modifications in the application requirements or in the programming process will be submitted to the customer. If possible, inhouse computer experts should be employed in writing this technical section, since they have an interest in achieving a successful application.

e. A definition of acceptable computer application software and what action on the part of the customer constitutes acceptance.

f. Expected conditions of contract performance. This includes which party prepares test data, how the customer approves test data and intermediate results, the time period desired for performance, the total cost and payment terms, guarantees of performance, and responsibility for latent defects. When a response shows a clearly defined schedule for programming, testing and approval of each detail step, this response suggest that the bidder has a grasp of the entire need and is likely to be able to perform satisfactorily. When PERT-COST, CPM or another scheduling technique is proposed by the bidder, the customer has a ready-made tool for monitoring progress during the course of the work.

g. A definition of terms and phrases used in the request.

h. A description of how disagreements and changes will be negotiated and settled.

When bids are received, the inhouse DP experts can assist the manager in evaluation. If the inhouse DP experts reviewing the proposals are associated with the inhouse computer center, they have the background to be certain that the proposed software will operate on the inhouse computer equipment. These same experts can counsel the manager on what constitutes an acceptable program, options to consider in establishing vendor responsibility for defects which are detected in use, how to appraise the qualifications of proposed programmer personnel, how to segment large applications projects for better control, and definition of technical terms and concepts.

If an inhouse DP expert is not available, the manager must be cautious about relying upon the vendor. The vendor's representative cannot be expected to know all the important characteristics of the manager's company, may not have enough legal training to understand the implications of the manager's needs, and, despite attempts to be objective, has an apparent self-interest in establishing the proposed contract. If the application is important and inhouse expertise is not available, the manager would do well to contract for expert advice from another firm which would not do the programming work. The costs that will be incurred for outside computer expertise should be measured against the importance of implementing on schedule and within a reasonable budget.

## E. SERVICE BUREAUS AND TIME-SHARING VENDORS

A service bureau or time-share vendor may be an excellent source of DP support. They will, however, differ widely in capacity and capability, reflecting differences in equipment, systems software, applications expertise, proprietary software, programming languages, and data processing support services, such as photocomposition interfaces, communications networks, programming, and systems analysis. As a result, selecting the best supplier to support a specific application is frequently a difficult task which cannot be judged successful until the proposed application has been operating effectively for some time.

### 1. Specialized Equipment

The equipment available at a service bureau or time share vendor may be similar to the equipment in the inhouse data center. Often, however, a specific vendor will possess computer equipment from several manufacturers or have special peripheral units, such as a high-speed page printer. The special equipment may be a reason to select that vendor.

## 2. Personnel Experience and Attitude

Vendor personnel often have a wide variety of experience in working with managers who have limited DP experience. This experience may be very different from the experience possessed by the inhouse data center's staff. The vendor's experience may include precisely the type of application that the manager wants to implement. However, it is often difficult for the manager to be certain that potential vendor's personnel have had appropriate experience. Vendor personnel usually appear to be highly cooperative in working with inexperienced managers and users. This attitude is fostered by the knowledge that satisfied customers keep the vendor in business and are the basis for raises and promotions. This attitude could influence some vendor personnel to promise more than they can deliver.

## 3. Proprietary Software

The largest service bureaus and time share vendors may have a significant collection of systems software and applications packages. This software may include packages that can be applied to almost every field. These vendors have an obvious interest in encouraging the manager to use their proprietary software, since this will tend to lock the manager into their service. The uniqueness of the vendor's software may also make it highly cost-effective for the manager's application. In any case, review and evaluate the software package before using it.

Consider the amount charged for the use of a proprietary package when determining the actual costs of using the service bureau or time-share vendor. If the actual costs can not be determined, the manager will not be able to make a meaningful comparison with the costs proposed by the inhouse data center. Future changes in the costs of operation or potential costs for revising the application are difficult to understand, if cost for software cannot be separated from cost of operation.

## 4. The Contracting Environment

Dealings with a service bureau or time share service can be established with a memorandum. As a practical matter, data processing services are such a complex product that simple memorandums have been replaced with formal written contracts, which may include several pages of small type and numerous clauses. When the application does not operate successfully, or when the vendor's charges are higher than the manager feels justified, these contract terms are important.

If the supplier makes an error in processing, the work is commonly redone without charge. However, this may be of little help to the user who must have work performed within a set time schedule. Suppliers normally take no responsibility for consequential losses due to delayed or incorrect processing, such as loss due to spoilage of perishable goods not shipped on time, or lost discounts offered on accounts payable.

If the manager wants to move an application from a vendor to the inhouse data center or to another vendor, processing and personnel costs will be incurred. In addition, the vendor's proprietary software may be expensive to replace.

Suppliers/vendors present their contract form-as standard. Since the supplier has prepared the contract and used it, they have reason to understand it. If the proposed application is considered critical in operation or costly, the manager should take the following steps in reviewing the proposed contract:

a. Obtain an inhouse legal opinion to determine the restrictions, limitations, and obligations, as well as the benefits proposed. How does the vendor define satisfactory performance? Will this definition meet the manager"s needs? What assurance does the vendor give that the services proposed will actually be supplied?
b. Have the DP expert review the contract. How will the manager be able to determine that the service promised is actually delivered?
c. The manager should review the legal findings and the DP expert's evaluation. If the proposed contract seems unreasonable or unclear, it should be discussed with the vendor's representative, and the manager should give serious consideration to using another vendor.

If a large contract is involved or if work is well within the vendor's capabilities, some compromise may be offered. If accepted, it should be put in writing and incorporated in the contract.

## 5. Service Bureau/Time-Share Contract Terms

There are many firms in the business of supplying DP services. Some of the important standard contract terms differ between vendors. Slight differences may be important to a manager. Comparison of essentially identical terms of two recent standard time-sharing contracts illustrates the difference between vendors. The first clause in each illustration are quoted with permission from the Boeing Computer Services Company. The second clauses are quoted by permission of a vendor requesting anonymity.

### a. The terms governing termination differ.

(1). "If no completion date is specified, either party may terminate this Agreement upon 30 days prior written notice."

(2). "After such period has elapsed, the Contract shall remain in force and effect unless terminated by either party at the end of any calendar month, on at least thirty (30) days prior written notice."

The termination clause in the first instance is 30 days, and in the second instance it is between 30 and 59 days, depending upon the day of the month. If the manager needs to discontinue the time-share vendors service to bring the application inhouse, the difference in time may be important. If the application is small and troublesome, the vendor may be anxious to discontinue service. Again the time difference may be important. In addition, the contract terms are to be interpreted by different state laws.

### b. Terms of payment differ.

(1). "Terms are net cash payable within 30 days after date of invoice,...."

(2). "In the event any invoice is not paid by Customer within ten (10) days after its date,...."

Strictly viewed, payment within ten days may not be administratively possible whereas thirty days is possible. Again, normal business practices may be to allow similar time periods, despite the written clauses. However, if your company can not get accounts payable processed quickly the vendor should be notified in advance. Sound business planning practices would include reaching a specific agreement on bill payment. This situation could be critical if some part of a manager's application is performed at various remote sites. For instance, a California site might find service cut off Friday afternoon, when no one can be contacted at the company's East coast headquarters to assure payment. When large widespread applications are involved, both the vendor and the user company should have specific points of contact to help operations move smoothly.

Vendors can not know exactly how a customer uses its computing facilities. As a result, standard contract forms minimize discussion of specific results. Full scale demonstrations and trial operations may be provided to eliminate questions of performance that might otherwise be raised by the manager.

Differences also exist in contract terms governing how and when rules and methods of operation may be changed, security features provided, express warranties on quality of services provided, and other items.

The variation in the clauses discussed may result in only minor differences in practice. Both of the vendors are organizations providing nationwide service. Such firms commonly make every effort to conduct operations in a cooperative manner to encourage additional business now and in the future. The manager should recognize the vendor's intention and resolve objectionable contract terms before problems arise.

If a manager intends to use a vendor's proprietary software, a separate agreement may be appended to the basic contract, or an entirely separate contract may be negotiated.

Certain vendor software may be provided at no-charge. This does not mean that the software is identical to software of the same name at another computer center. The manager should expect the software to be different, so that a complex sophisticated application might not be easily operated at another center without considerable cost.

**SUMMARY**

Implementation of an application can be performed using an inhouse data processing center and inhouse programmers or performed by contract with outside vendors, as well as with combinations of inhouse support and outside vendors. When packaged software may be used, it is a preferred option. Contracting for custom-developed software is an especially difficult process compared to contracting to operate an application. All vendor contract terms are not identical, but should be acceptable before the manager commits the company.

# 5

# Installing the application

## A. INTRODUCTION

The installation process begins with the preliminary approval and installation of the equipment and software, and is completed with the operational acceptance of the application. Other major steps in the process include site preparation, user training, and operational training. All previous expenditures would be wasted if the installation is not successful. This chapter describes the roles and responsibilities of the manager who directs the installation and the steps in the installation process.

## B. THE INSTALLATION MANAGER'S ROLE

The manager's role in installation includes both planning and operational aspects. The planning efforts build upon existing plans. It is assumed that the necessary computer programs for the application will be provided by a DP expert, either at an inhouse data center or at a service bureau or time-sharing vendor. Operational efforts focus on directing and coordinating the installation of the equipment and software, and conclude with acceptance testing and approval. The effort involved in a successful installation is a function of the size and complexity of the application.

## 1. Planning Efforts

Begin planning with a review and evaluation of installation planning parameters developed during the earlier general planning. Update and revise this earlier general planning, then determine and add the specifics. This detailed installation plan should center attention on planning the user site, training of users, and establishing the application's acceptance and approval process. For instance, define hardware for installation at the user site (or sites) and order it, so that it may arrive in time to meet the planned operational date. Complete plans for the general location of user terminal equipment, design of special forms, and contracting for major building changes.

## 2. Operational Responsibility

Operational efforts involve reviewing and coordinating the completion of the installation plan. Major construction must be completed prior to equipment installation. User training must be provided. If training is to be provided by contract, determine that a contract has been placed, attendees selected, and classes scheduled.

Communications lines must be installed and operational before terminals can be connected. Terminal equipments may require stands or special types of desks. Orders for all equipment and service should specify early delivery dates, so that possible delays will not affect the total installation plan. Although terminal equipment may have been ordered, contact the vendor to determine that the equipment has actually been shipped. When several sites are involved, check the implementation status at each site to insure that overall installation dates will be met. Review and check the testing of software and hardware acording to the original application goals and objectives. Modify the testing plan as necessary to meet the application goals.

### 3. Level of Effort

The planning process is the same for both large and small applications. However, the effort required depends upon the size and importance of the application to the manager and the company. The application size should be measured by the number of sites, terminals, and users involved. The importance of the application is determined by the manager, based primarily on estimates of costs and benefits.

## C. USER SITE REQUIREMENTS

User site planning involves quantifying and organizing the site requirements. The large application with numerous sites requires more planning effort. Quantify such things as the number of sites, the various types of physical environments, the geographic distribution and clustering of sites within an area, the number of types of terminals involved, and the security and backup required.

### 1. Site Installation Factors

Planning for the user site installations should be started by listing all the pertinent assumptions. A list of assumptions for an application dealing with finished goods inventory could include:

a. Six sites are involved.

b. Sites 1 and 2 are located in major manufacturing facilities in small towns.

c. Sites 1 and 2 will be located in dusty, noisy manufacturing areas.

d. Glass-enclosed office space must be constructed in sites 1 and 2 to protect the equipment from heat and dust.

e. The small town locations are 450 miles apart.

f. Sites 3-6 are located in large cities.

g. Sites 3-6 will be located in office areas in warehouse facilities.

h. Cities are located 800 miles from the manufacturing plants and 200 miles from each other.

i. The application involves installation of small terminals that are used to enter orders and to print out shipping instructions.

j. All terminals must be connected to a computer center at site 1.

k. Each terminal must have a 1200 bps dial-up communications connection.

l. Communications will be required for about 1 hour per day, except for sites 1 and 2, which will have about 2 hours per day spread out over 8 hours.

m. The communications service will be provided by a packet carrier.

n. Each terminal must have equipment for data communications.

o. All terminals operate on 110 volts AC. The terminal manufacturer specifies a separate 20 amp service for each machine.

p. All sites must have a supply of prenumbered multipart shipping forms. These are a special continuous form.

q. All terminals must have a supply of two part continuous paper for recording data entry information.

r. Each site will have a CRT-type terminal with a typewriter style keyboard and 30 cps printer.

s. Terminal printers must be capable of printing sixpart forms.

t. Terminals require special ribbons and plastic daisy wheels for the printer.

u. Each terminal site must have on hand eight boxes of paper stock plus ribbons and extra print wheels.

v. Site 1 and 6 will be installed first because they have space and power available without any major renovations.

w. Sites 1, 2, and 6 will have two terminals to insure backup equipment in case of equipment problems.

x. All sites will have basic power protection equipment.

y. The first application testing will involve the two terminals and the computer center at site 1.

These assumptions should be changed and modified to fit the specific application. The various steps in planning the user site physical installation plan are illustrated in Figure 5-1, Site Installation Physical Planning Schedule.

FIGURE 5-1 Site Installation Physical Planning Schedule

| | Week 1 | 2 | 3 | 4 | 5 | 6 | 7 | 8 | 9 | 10 | 11 | 12 | 13 |
|---|---|---|---|---|---|---|---|---|---|---|---|---|---|
| Place Contracts | | | | | | | | | | | | | |
| Communications | * | | | | | | | | | | | | |
| Construction | * | | | | | | | | | | | | |
| Supplies | * | | | | | | | | | | | | |
| Physical Installations | | | | | | | | | | | | | |
| Sites 1 and 6 | | | * | | | | | | | | | | |
| Sites 2, 3, 4, 5 | | | | | | | * | | | | | | |
| Test Equipment Operation | | | | | | | | | | | | | |
| Site 1 | | | | * | | | | | | | | | |
| Site 2 | | | | | | | | | | | | | |
| Sites 3, 4, 5, 6 | | | | | | | | | | | | | |

## 2. Backup for User Sites

Manual systems may be used as backup for an application because of their generally low cost, although in many instances, they cannot provide the speed, accuracy, or subtlety to handle a complex application. If a manual system is used, backup for a sophisticated computer application may be limited to storing input data documents, until the computer system is back in operation. In some applications, such as order entry, a manual system might be used to record all sales, but to summarize and support billing only for major orders.

If the backup system is to be automated, it may require additional computer terminals, access to another computer, and protection of the computer applications software and the data files. A number of alternatives are possible. One increasingly available form of computer backup is an inhouse word processing unit or a small computer available at the user's location. Such small equipment may not have sufficient speed or capacity to process more than a few of the transactions involved, or to do more than a limited amount of processing with each transaction that is handled.

Minor terminal failures can be corrected by maintenance. Major failures are resolved by replacement of the terminal. In critical applications, a second terminal may be installed nearby. If work volumes are high or time of data entry or report output is important, provide a second terminal at the same site. A second terminal provides good backup for the primary terminal, if sufficient time is available to do the necessary work on that second terminal.

The computer application may be backed up on another computer system. A simplified version of the application system may be used on another computer system. If the user has a large company computer center, the software for the application may be copied on another computer in that computer center. If the application is run at an outside timeshare vendor, they will typically have the software available on another computer at the same or another computer center. If their computer centers are directly connected, they can substitute the backup system for the failed system without the user's being aware of a failure.

An important application may be fully backed up by maintaining a copy of all software and data files, storing them away from the main site, and having arrangements to operate the application at another computer center, time-share vendor or service bureau that has the exact equipment needed.

Except for the manual system, backup facilities at the user site commonly require data communications to connect terminals to a host computer or to other users. If private wired lines are used, provide a second set for a backup terminal. If telephone lines are used, a delay from one week to perhaps two months must be expected in installation, so that the additional lines should be ordered now, rather than when an emergency occurs.

## D. TRAINING

No matter how carefully an application is designed, its success depends on the people who actually use the terminals. Training is important because new terminal users may not know how to use the equipment. Training should cover four areas: basic terminal operation, application use instructions, terminal problems and solutions, and supply and maintenance procedures.

### 1. Basic Terminal Operation

The terminal manufacturer may supply an instruction booklet or pamphlet along with each device. These booklets often explain every detail of operation, including some which are not important to the application. In other instances, the booklet does not provide enough information, especially for users who have not had previous computer experience. A supplementary information sheet is frequently used to summarize the most important operating details in terms that are chosen to fit the user's requirements.

### 2. Application Instructions

Each application has its specific method of performance, including steps to be taken when making an entry, correcting an entry, inserting a change in existing data, and recognizing errors or failures in the application system or the terminal equipment.

Specify the information to be included in a proper data entry. It must include such items as the customer name, customer representative, customer ship to address, customer billing address, salesperson, date of required delivery, item numbers, item quantities, discount schedule to apply, and reference to existing contract. Explain the content and format of each data element: the customer name should be the name of the local customer organization, rather than the corporate name, so that the organization is clearly identified. If a different name is used for billing, that name should be appended with the notation, "BILL TO." The item number should be three digits, preceded by a two-character alphabetic code. All acceptable item numbers will be listed in a Part Number Cross Reference listing.

Detailed instructions may be needed to guide a user through complex testing operations that could destroy data or affect the program, if mishandled. These application instructions and materials should be used in the first location to implement the application, since there are often changes needed that can only be discovered by experience.

**3. Terminal Problems and Solutions**

Terminals may have initial mechanical or electronic failure, parts wear can cause erratic terminal operation behavior, data communications service may be marginal, and new users can make mistakes. Any of these problems can interfere with an otherwise successful application. Even after training, some user personnel are nervous about making mistakes. The installation manager should assist them in performing quick problem identification and effective corrective action by providing a short, uncomplicated troubleshooting memo or, if appropriate, a manual. Such a guide should contain all necessary information in an easy-to-use format, along with names and telephone numbers of service personnel. The guide assists in correcting the many trivial, but disabling, problems that occur in a new application, and expedites contacting the proper service people for more complicated problems.

**4. Supply and Maintenance Procedures**

Applications require supplies, such as ribbons, tapes, and forms. Terminal equipment requires periodic maintenance and repair. If proper supplies are unavailable, or the equipment fails, the application is halted. Order supplies in advance and store where they are protected from misuse. If a user terminal is operated by two or more people, each one should know where supplies are kept, as well as how to identify maintenance problems and the person to contact. Procedures should be established to eliminate possible supply outages and to insure that maintenance is notified quickly. A typical approach to handling supplies is to prepare a list with instructions for reordering and tape same to the supply cabinet. The phone number of the service contact can be marked on a self-stick label and taped to the side of the terminal. If the terminal is heavily used, it is common to have one or two of the heaviest users act as key operators, do all the ordering of supplies, and initiate all contacts with maintenance. Their names and telephone numbers should also be taped on the terminal. Large applications with many identical terminals often have personnel from a DP group assigned to handle all service and supplies. A new application that uses existing terminals may be able to utilize the procedures that already exist.

## E. APPLICATION ACCEPTANCE AND APPROVAL

Despite careful planning, problems normally arise in achieving a fully acceptable installation. These problems include equipment that may not function as anticipated, insufficient or incorrect supplies, users who do not understand the equipment or the application, or errors in the application programs. In addition, it is possible that some details, unnoticed or apparently unimportant in the development or general implementation, are actually important to obtain an economic and effective solution. Installation problems should be solved and needed changes incorporated as part of the plan for acceptance testing, prior to seeking a formal management approval. Acceptance testing is comprised of three parts:

a. establishing testing objectives,
b. developing appropriate tests, and
c. scheduling and performing the tests.

The effort involved depends upon the importance and scope of the application.

### 1. Acceptance Testing Objectives

Acceptance testing is used to determine that the application, as installed, actually does everything it was originally intended to do. Determining acceptance testing objectives is a two-part problem. The first part is to insure that the objectives as stated are acceptable to management at this time. The second part is to define the objectives in terms of specific actions. Technical quality in a computer application is not a guarantee of an effective solution. No matter how carefully the original objectives have been established, requirements may have changed during the period between application request and application installation. As the time for acceptance testing nears, the application objectives should be resubmitted for final management approval.

The installation manager should review the objectives with the requesting manager, who will then have an opportunity to reconfirm the objectives. If the original application incorporated compromises in output report format or frequency, user training, interface to other computer applications, and so forth, these compromises can be discussed with concerned parties to minimize potential disagreements after the installation has been completed.

This review and reconfirmation technique gives the requesting manager improved control and flexibility during the installation process and may be important in critical applications. If application testing shows that results are not up to management expectation, action can be taken to improve the solution. If results are as originally designed, but are not fully satisfactory in practice, the manager has an opportunity to determine that design changes must be made before the application should be considered satisfactory.

Applications testing should be aimed at:

a. producing reports based upon live data,
b. verifying that report formats and contents are correct and complete, as required by the application design specification.
c. verifying that operating costs and benefits received are as planned,
d. verifying that time schedules for collecting, processing, and reporting information are being met, and
e. verifying that the information service provided is a good solution to the actual problem.

Figure 5-2, Acceptance Testing Evaluation, illustrates some of the factors that might be included as acceptance testing objectives for an application that is concerned with setting inventory levels. In this example, minimizing the cost of the product inventory investment is contrasted to the loss of profits when an order cannot be filled. This type of application may be important to any company that has a large percentage of its assets invested in inventory, especially if the costs of money are considered high and/or seasonal sales patterns are involved. In this example, assume that a few terminals are used to enter data at random during the day using communications lines to a computer located elsewhere. Also assume that the applications programming software consists of several programs to collect and edit the input as received, to provide intermediate output reports twice daily, and to provide revised financial projections every morning. This scenario has elements common to a large number of possible applications. The evaluation data shown in Figure 5-2 must be developed from performing acceptance tests.

FIGURE 5-2 Acceptance Testing Evaluation

APPLICATION:______________________________

| Factor | Evaluation |
|---|---|
| 1. Data on orders received, line items and quantity | Data is received from two terminals in warehouse. Data is consistently accurate and correlates with inventory counts and receiving reports. |
| 2. Projected cost of funds information from Controller | Information input 5:30 P.M. every evening. |
| 3. Application program is satisfactory | Proprietary planning model is used by vendor. Reports to Controller 9 A.M. every day. |
| 4. Output formats | Reports show high, low, and recommended inventory level as planned. |
| 5. Costs and budgets | 10% less than original target, due to use of proprietary software. |
| 6. Cost-effectiveness | Inventory investment reduced by $400,000 with no noticable loss of sales. Loss due to overage stock cut from $100,000 to $20,000 annually. |

Note: All information is for illustrative purposes only.

## 2. Acceptance Tests

A management objective is often a general statement. Testing must be specific. Calculations must be correct, data must be processed without errors, erroneous data must be properly filtered out and corrected. Each test should have carefully defined inputs and required output results. For instance, if a calculation is involved, a given set of input transactions must result in specific output values. If logical processing is involved, a series of transactions representing every logical alternative should be used as input and results should be exactly as planned. Figure 5-3 lists some of the acceptance testing that could be performed to provide the information to evaluate an application.

FIGURE 5-3 Acceptance Testing Measurements

APPLICATION: ______________________________

| Factor | Measurement |
|---|---|
| 1. Data input quality | Count errors in data. Classify by terminal and operator. Cross classify by type. |
| 2. Computer edit | Insert known erroneous data at a terminal to determine that it is identified and rejected according to the program design objective. |
| 3. Program operation | The application program has operated without problems for a period of 30 calendar days. |
| 4. Program operating time and cost | The program requires 40 minutes of processing time daily at a cost of $146. Application has a planned annual cost of $35,000. |
| 5. Input terminal reliability | Count and classify number of machine failures and human errors to determine terminal reliability and ease of use. |
| 6. Output | Reports are prepared in exactly the specified formats. They are available on time to the Controller and to the Inventory Manager. |

## 3. Scheduling and Performing Acceptance Testing

Acceptance testing must take place as soon as possible. The testing schedule should begin with checking live terminal operation with small quantities of known sample data that can be processed and discarded. When terminal and software operation is acceptable, actual operating data should then be entered through the terminals. If the data is critical or sensitive, extra effort should be placed on counting the number of input messages and keeping copies to verify later that the processing was correct. Each and every failure or error should be recorded, so that it can be matched against a corrective action. Frequently, a certain type of failure recurs, since the corrective action taken by the computer program did not solve the problem. Written records help to identify problems and assist in pinpointing the necessary correction process.

## 4. Management Approval

Management approval may range from a casual and unstructured process to a highly formal affair, complete with a written memorandum and a meeting of high level managers. The approval process reflects:

a. the importance of the applicaton to the company,
b. the importance of the application to the manager, and
c. the company characteristics (size, age, style of management, industry practices).

At the minimum, a memo of acceptance should be prepared by the installation manager to the manager requiring the application. Such memos are often omitted because an oral notification is thought to be adequate. The manager requiring the application should insist on a written memo for all but the most trivial application to:

a. clearly determine responsibilities,
b. establish acceptable completion dates,
c. insure that full and complete notice is available, and
d. insure that all users and other concerned parties, especially those in remote locations or different parts of the organization, are informed.

If an acceptance memo is difficult to prepare, the

FIGURE 5-4 Application Acceptance Memorandum Format

FROM: (Name and Title)

TO: (Name and Title)

SUBJECT: (Name of Application)

CONTENTS:

(Abbreviation of Application Title, Acronym, if any

Date Testing was Accepted

Reference to Specifications involved--name each reference document or memorandum

Specify where Documentation is Stored

Identify the DP Technical Contact

Identify the DP Operational Contact

State where the Application is now being run--the name and location of a time-share service, a local service bureau, or a corporate data center

Describe the locations in which the Application is now being Operated: which offices and which office locations)

cc: (Names of Concerned parties with location and organization)

manager should consider that the entire application installation process is likely to be poorly understood by concerned parties who are not involved in the day-to-day installation problems. The basic acceptance memo should give the formal title of the application, as well as any other short title or acronym used to identify the application. It should also reference the documentation used and prepared, including who prepared it and when, and where copies are available. List the principal concerned parties, their locations, and organizations (identifying the computer center supplying the service), the organization and office locations at which terminals are located, contacts for repair and maintenance service on terminals, contacts for revision and rescheduling of application processing priority and updating of the application design.

Figure 5-4 illustrates the format of a basic acceptance memo. Further details will be appropriate in some circumstances.

## F. SUMMARY

A successful computer application requires appropriate and cost-effective computer programs. The programs alone are rarely enough to complete an application, especially if the user requires terminals or special forms or reports. These and other details are often a major portion of an application, and when they are major, their successful installation is a necessity. Except for small applications and special circumstances, an installation manager is commonly appointed to coordinate this effort, because of the number of details.

# 6

# Conducting a management audit

## A. INTRODUCTION

An independent review of progress and techniques may be useful during the development of a computer application. A critical review of the application is highly desirable for every completed application. These reviews are traditionally thought of as audits, and focus on compliance with accounting standards. However, the subject matter involved is better appraised from a general management viewpoint, which is broader in scope.

This chapter contains a description of the various audit objectives, an explanation of the auditing process, special audit areas that may be involved in computer applications, and the audit report.

## B. AUDIT OBJECTIVES

Every application should be carefully reviewed to determine how closely it has met its original objectives. A number of specific objectives should be considered from a general management perspective, as well as from the view of the manager who requested the application. Objectives to be reviewed are classified under six headings for this discussion:

a. Operating Rules and Economics,
b. Internal Controls,
c. Input Specifications,
d. Manual Procedures,
e. Exceptions Processing, and
f. Results vs. Objectives.

## 1. Operating Rules and Economics

Does the processing comply with the operating rules of the computer center that will run the application? If not, what is the effect? As implemented, the application may use more computer resources than customarily allowed: more high-speed main memory, more disks, more tapes. When this occurs, the processing is often continued, but may be subjected to substantial delays in processing and be charged a premium rate as a penalty. The delays imposed can stretch a time-critical job from completion in seconds to completion in minutes, perhaps losing much of the benefit of the anticipated fast response: delayed calculation and reporting for foreign exchange rates and trading would result in delayed buying or selling of foreign exchange at the bank or brokerage firm which means that less favorable prices will be accepted.

Is the computer processing efficient and economical for this application? When the application is planned, the cost of computer resources is the cost at that time. However, new equipment and software are frequently being installed, so that the application is then operated in an improved and changed environment: large amounts of disk storage may be much cheaper now than when the application was originally designed. An application that was designed to minimize the amount of disk storage because of costs, might now be redesigned to reduce cost by increasing the use of disk storage.

## 2. Internal Controls

Has the application been designed to incorporate internal controls that prevent error and deliberate tampering during normal operation? A financial routine that allows overdue accounts to be dropped from the normal processing cycle can be misused. Strict controls, such as dollar totals, customer number or account controls, transaction count controls, and automatic reporting of all exceptions, are commonly used to detect and identify such irregularities. Necessary corrective steps should be outlined in written form, so that prompt action can be taken. Typically, an individual who is outside of the operating organization will be assigned specific responsibility for taking corrective action.

### 3. Input Data Specifications

Does the actual data input to the application meet the specification? An application design commonly assumes that the input data will meet a given set of characteristics. Some of the characteristics include the numeric range of the data (between 1000 and 9999), the format of the data (the data will always be presented in the form of twelve characters, in which the first four are alphabetic, except that the letters I, O, Q, U and X are not permitted). Once the application has been implemented, and operational data flows through the system, exceptions appear (although the first four letters are alphabetic, the letter T is also not permitted, and any entry with the letters R or S will be processed, but must be identified as an exception).

Data input changes, such as more characters being required in a data field or record, may cause considerable trouble in operating the application as planned. The application may require a change, if it is to continue to be effective, and in some instances, the change may be costly. If data communications is involved in the application (data is transmitted between remote field offices and division or corporate headquarters), changes in data input specifications may create operating problems. If data to be transmitted includes larger records than originally planned, the time allowed for data transmission may be insufficient, so that data would be lost or garbled in transmission.

### 4. Manual Procedures

How efficient and economical are related manual processing procedures? If all input data was keypunched bcause large amounts were handwritten, the situation may be changed, because data is now being received in typed form with fewer errors. The process of batching input data, sending to keypunch, and physically delivering punched cards may be replaced by using an optical character reading unit to read and enter input data directly onto a magnetic tape or disk. A different set of manual handling procedures is needed. In many instances, less radical changes are needed in manual procedures to reflect the effects of increasing volumes of transactions, improved quality of data, and different methods of conducting business.

## 5. Exceptions Processing

Both exceptions processing rules and the handling of exceptions processing must be appraised. Should the rules for exceptions processing be changed? The volume and frequency of exceptions estimated in designing an application is often found to be different when the application is in operation. A rule establishing a ceiling for purchasing without formal paperwork may be unreasonable, because inflation has increased prices. The results of this rule may generate a long exceptions report when only a few items have significance for management. An overly long exceptions report also suggests that the application is incurring reporting costs that can be eliminated. An exception which was trivial and infrequent when the application was originally designed may have changed and is now important.

Does processing follow the rules which were established? Applications that control the flow of money or goods generally have carefully designed exceptions processing to minimize errors in processing and to discourage and detect fraud or embezzlement. The exceptions processing involved is normally subjected to some changes as programmers improve the application. Unfortunately, the processing may have had some deficiencies in its first implementation, there may be some new type of exception which has developed, or the processing may have been changed so that some exceptions are undetected or unreported.

## 6. Results vs. Objectives

When an application is implemented, the manager may assume that his stated objectives have been met. This is not always the case for many reasons, including:

a. changes in objectives after the application was completed,

b. redefinition of objectives which were not fully explained or understood by the computer experts,
c. a deficiency in the initial application design, and
d. a change in the application after the application was originally installed.

The only way to find out if the application meets its objectives completely is to compare the results against each objective. Once an application has been implemented, it may be continued after it has lost many of its benefits, unless it is reviewed.

Did this application do the job at the expected costs? The original estimated costs for developing the application and the estimated operating costs should be compared to actual costs. Significant differences should be appraised to determine that they are reasonable and justified, and to locate important changes that will affect proposed applications or applications currently being developed.

## C. PERFORMING THE AUDIT

Performing an audit may be considered a nine-step process:

1. Plan the audit process.
2. Establish the audit scope.
3. Set audit standards.
4. Develop an understanding of the application, typically by reviewing available documentation.
5. Select appropriate audit techniques.
6. Review data.
7. Review outputs.
8. Review special audit areas, if required.
9. Prepare and present a final audit report.

Proper performance of the audit compares application results to the original objectives and identifies differences.

### 1. Audit Plan

Begin every audit by preparing an audit plan that organizes the effort, establishes the techniques and approaches, and insures that audit objectives are met.

The audit plan organizes the effort by establishing a series of tasks to be performed. Identify each task, such as verify list of accounts receivable. Specify the work to be done, such as send out letters to all accounts, verify all accounts over $100,000 by telephone calls and visits. Define the performance period, such as the verification task starts within one week and will be completed within four weeks. Assign personnel to the audit task, such as an auditor and a senior auditor. The audit plan also establishes some method to determine which audited items are critical to a successful operation and what relative importance each of these items bears: misspelling a salesperson's or manager's name is annoying, but incorrect calculations may be costly. This process allows the audit to guide the manager in correcting or improving the critical items immediately, while avoiding or minimizing the expense of correcting less important audit deficiencies.

How will the application audit be conducted? If an inexperienced person will perform the audit, the results may be one-sided or superficial. An experienced audit supervisor should be involved to establish the audit project and its methods, and to review its performance and completion. The additional personnel costs invariably result in a better audit.

## 2. Audit Scope

The audit performed in conjunction with a specific application may have a number of different objectives. It may be for general management purposes, or for a more specific reason, such as security, a privacy review, risk management, contingency or disaster planning, measuring/improving equipment utilization, or measuring/improving application effectiveness.

## 3. Auditing Standards

All computer applications should be audited to meet specific minimum standards for accuracy and completeness. These standards commonly appear in the form of a checklist or sets of checklists for evaluating each audit objective: design process, exceptions processing, efficiency and economy, effectiveness in meeting design objectives. These standards assist in the detection and correction of application deficiencies and failures.

## 4. Auditing Techniques

Review an application for the presence of audit trails, and test to verify that transactions are properly processed. Normally, the validity of this approach depends upon the availability and use of good documentation. Even the best-planned documentation frequently lacks updating changes, or may not have all the expected content. If the application is complex, there is a possibility of incomplete or outdated documentation.

A more sophisticated approach involves auditing through the computer system. This approach may take several forms, including use of a general purpose audit program to manipulate and extract data, and use of special test decks to verify that correct transactions are processed as expected, and improper entries are detected and reported as errors or exceptions.

A major area for review of an application is the documentation. Review of the documentation provides a guide as to what the application is designed to do and how it accomplishes these objectives. The amount of documentation, its accuracy, and its completeness must be considered. Is all essential application documentation available: statement of objectives, cost/benefit analysis, feasibility analysis? Is the documentation submitted complete and properly approved? Is test data described and available to be processed according to the documentation?

## 5. Data Review

The input data, the output data, and temporary working files of data may be checked for completeness and validity. Typical questions to be asked by the auditor in performing the review include:

a. Input Data
   1. What conditions identify an input as incomplete (sales invoice number missing)?
   2. Are incomplete inputs properly marked for exceptions processing? (Do they appear in an exceptions listing, identified as incomplete or otherwise explained?)
   3. What conditions identify an input as invalid (incorrect sales invoice, sales representative or product codes, or the product price does not match standard sales price)?

4. Are invalid inputs properly marked for exceptions processing? (do they appear in an exceptions listing noted as invalid with an explanation?)
5. Are the sources of incomplete/invalid input identified for correction (the input terminal, the sales number, the sales branch)?
6. Are the sources of incomplete/invalid input quantified to direct the correcting effort? (Are counts given to identify the primary sources and the major types of errors?)

b. Output Data
   1. Are all expected items of data present (sales invoice number)?
   2. Are data items within expected values (sales commissions do not exceed $5,000 per sales representative)?

c. Working Data Files
   Do files reflect changes expected when new data is input (sales representative's cumulative sales dollars are increased by amount of sale; accounts receivable balances are increased by sales amount)?

### 6. Output Review

The basic documentation review and data review serve as learning steps for the auditor, prior to performing an appraisal of the application outputs. The auditor's first step in reviewing the outputs is to obtain a listing of all outputs and the specification for each. With this information and background, the auditor should answer questions including:

a. Do the output reports meet the original specification? Does each item of data called for appear in the output?
b. Are outputs produced and available on schedule?
c. Do the outputs satisfy management's needs? Are the users satisfied? What modifications are suggested and why?

## D. SPECIAL AUDIT AREAS

Computer applications may be developed and implemented in a variety of ways, which may lead to special audit approaches. Special approaches include performing an interim audit for approval of a new application before it is implemented, auditing a computer application which replaces a manual system, auditing packaged software, and auditing that involves a service bureau.

## 1. The Interim Audit

Some applications are considered highly critical because cash or merchandise is involved, or perhaps because of their importance to an organization. In such instances, a concerned manager may request an audit to minimize the possibility of a future operational failure, or for other reasons, such as gauging the impact of the new application on cash float. The objectives of this audit should be stated before it is started, so that the proper questions will be asked.

The questions to be asked by the auditor will be largely answered by a documentation review. The audit itself may be directed toward a review of internal control to see if and how such controls are incorporated. Exceptions rules, exceptions processing, manual processing, or cost-effectiveness may also be evaluated in critical applications.

## 2. The Manual System Conversion

As a company grows, manual applications may become inadequate and will be replaced by automated systems. This situation is common, and may not be given adequate attention, because many of the personnel involved are presumably responsible and knowledgable. As a matter of fact, personnel familiar with the manual system can and do make honest mistakes working with the new system. Because honest mistakes are inevitable and new automated applications may have undiscovered weakness, applications that affect critical items may be manipulated. Typical applications that fall into this category may include expense account report approval, disposal of surplus property, purchase of low value items or transfer of small items. If the application controls the movement of money or goods, it is a candidate for audit. Audits of this type have two common objectives: detect errors that may have occurred, especially during the transition period, and find out if adequate internal controls exist in the automated application. If errors occurred during the transition, the audit is concerned with determining how they occurred, and if they have been corrected.

### 3. Auditing Packaged Software

As packaged software (computer programs) becomes more available and is widely used, it becomes an increasingly important part of many computer applications. The auditor should review this software for operation according to the vendor's specification and the application specification. When packaged software is involved, focus on present or potential limitations in the software. Questions to be answered include:

a. What are the copyright and licensing restrictions which may limit the use of this software and may affect the application: is its use limited to a single computer system or to computer systems only at this location? Can this software be used on another manufacturer's computer system?

b. What are copyright and licensing restrictions involving customizing or modifying this package to meet special needs of the manager? Can the using company customize the software to meet special needs of its own? Can this customized version be copyrighted by the using company to retain a competitive advantage?

c. What is the vendor's responsibility for errors in processing resulting from imperfections in the software? How will the vendor correct latent defects in the software package and upgrade documentation?

### 4. Auditing Service Bureaus

If the application is partially or totally performed by a service bureau or time-sharing vendor, to what extent should and can that supplier be audited? If the application is considered critical, the best interest of the corporation are served by performing an audit. However, there is an immediate problem in doing so, since the service bureau or time-sharing vendor is a separate legal entity, and may be processing computer work for a number of other companies. Any audits performed at the service bureau or time-sharing vendor facilities will be under the control of that supplier, so that the user must rely largely upon the supplier's policies and procedures. When using a service bureau or time-sharing vendor, the critical application should be designed to be checked and audited by embedding internal controls such as counts, totals, reports upon completion of steps. These internal controls should signal an error or problem immediately. The audit trail should be planned to trace the transaction processing and locate the source of the failure: it should determine that the failure is in the vendor's software processing, in vendor manual procedures, or in the using company procedures, in the data input. If sensitive information is involved, the supplier's policies and procedures need special review to determine what problems may occur in processing the application, and how these potential problems may be avoided or overcome. A meeting between the vendor, the auditor, and the manager may be desirable as part of this special review.

## E. THE AUDIT REPORT

The results of an application audit appear in the formal audit report. The report reflects both a formal review against a set of standards, as well as the philosophy of the personnel concerned. The effectiveness of the audit report is enhanced by careful organization and appropriate presentation.

### 1. Audit Report Philosophy

The audit team may view their task in different ways. The team may serve as a judge ruling on the value of the application to the corporation, with the concerned manager being regarded as an interested party. In other instances, its attention is focused on identifying inadequacy, incompetence, undue cost in design or operation, and other negative aspects. The audit team may also take the position of an enlightened manager, in which it identifies deficiencies, recommends and institutes corrections and improvements, and calculates benefits. An audit may be undertaken to determine compliance with accounting standards. A management audit approach appears to be preferable, since it implies use of management standards, as well as an independent judgment. Figure 6-1 lists some of the advantages and disadvantages of the management audit.

FIGURE 6-1 Management Audit

| Benefits | Shortcomings |
|---|---|
| Sample of processing results is inadequate | Sampling all characteristics is too costly. |
| Reasonable overview of application operation | Not cost-effective in many small or straightforware applications |
| Judgment made by an outside, independent group | Requires auditors with EDP training |
| Justification of managers plans and approach | Widely distributed applications are often poorly audited, because of costs of review at each location. |
| Opportunity for manager to modify and further improve is based on experience | May require additional EDP expertise on manager's part to be of any use |
| Improvements in service are broadly based, rather than derived from a narrow viewpoint | The broad viewpoint may delay other important EDP work and may incur cost for use of EDP equipment |

The organization responsible for the development and implementation of the application may take different positions regarding an audit. A common position is to provide the minimum of documentation and information to the audit team to reduce expected potentially negative comments. A second position taken is to supply all material when and as requested by the audit team. Some applications affect a large number of people, and in these instances, the responses of the application users are not necessarily consistent, nor necessarily a reflection of their manager's attitudes. The philosophy evidenced by the audit team during the course of the audit, as well as during previous audits, is commonly accepted as indicating the philosophy which will underly the finished audit report.

## 2. Audit Report Format

The audit report should be prepared as a formal technical report. Its contents should be well organized and presented, using a clear, lucid writing style. In some instances writing style, organization, and contents may be established by a company policy or standard.

Figure 6-2 outlines the general content of an audit report, with sections for Introduction and Overview, Audit Conduct, Audit Findings, and Recommendations. Figure 6-3 illustrates a cover letter format that is suitable for most audits.

FIGURE 6-2 Application Audit Report Format

AUDIT REPORT ON (Application Title) (Date Prepared) (Audit Identification Number, if any)

I. INTRODUCTION AND OVERVIEW

A. Identify the application that was audited.

B. Provide background information on the organizations involved in developing theapplication and special application features.

C. Describe the application objectives.

II. AUDIT CONDUCT

A. Explain the size, composition, and background of the audit team members in relation to this audit.

B. Discuss the objectives to be satisfied by the audit.

C. Describe the auditing procedure that was followed, including use of sample data, verifying input data, review of exceptions processing, and examination of applications results against design requirements. Include, as appropriate, lists of audit questions used.

FIGURE 6-2 Application Audit Report Format (continued)

III. AUDIT FINDINGS

A. Describe each major audit finding, indicating compliance or noncompliance with the original specifications.

B. Indicate the extent to which each major audit finding was based upon limited test samples, actual performance over months, etc.

C. Discuss the extent and depth of ongoing changes that relate to major audit findings.

IV. RECOMMENDATIONS

A. Arrange list of recommendations, with most critical items first.

B. Explain each recommendation, indicating expected costs, benefits, organizations, and equipment/procedures.

FIGURE 6-3 Audit Report Cover Letter Format

SUBJECT: AUDIT REPORT ON (Application Title) Date Submitted

________________

The audit report attached represents a management audit of the (Name of Application) performed between (Start Date) and (Ending Date). This audit was authorized by (Give name of Organization, Individual Requesting, or Corporate Policy that requires).

| APPROVING MANAGER | AUDIT TEAM LEADER (Manager) |
|---|---|
| (Name) | (Name) |
| | AUDIT TEAM MEMBERS |
| | (List) |

## 3. Audit Report Presentation

More benefits are achieved if an audit report is designed to report on constructive action rather than list deficiencies. To achieve this result, a preliminary draft should be provided and discussed on an informal basis with the appropriate managers before the finished report is presented. The finished report should include a subsection within the findings to discuss corrective changes and improvements in process. Every presentation should report both positive and negative aspects of the review. A presentation with a strong positive tone will have negative findings more easily accepted.

The presentation of the finished audit report should be scheduled as soon as a reasonable audit completion date is established. Often, the presentation date and the information supplied will influence a number of management decisions related to further automation, changes in the direction of automation, and restructuring of corporate functions and responsibilities.

The style of an audit report presentation must be determined by the subject matter, legal implications, audience, and the person(s) making the presentation. A formal printed report, with sufficient copies for all attendees, plus additional working copies, is desirable. Preparation of the report typically involves typing the document and reproducing it with inhouse offset or photocopy equipment to maintain privacy and control.

The report may be presented using charts, 35mm slides, or transparency film. Often the presentation is a copy of the report outline with some additional special points expanded. Distribute copies of the report after the presentation to avoid having attendees reading during the presentation.

Those attending the audit presentation should include concerned parties, such as the operational application manager, the DP expert, higher level management, members of the Controller's department, the Director of the auditing function, managers of related applications, and user supervisors concerned with input of data or use of output products. Other appropriate management personnel and the audit staff should attend.

The results of the audit may have legal implications: a valuable asset has been identified, copyright problems or opportunities have been identified, or fraud, embezzlement, or a violation of government privacy laws has been discovered. In such instances, the corporate legal counsel should be notified as soon as these implications are discovered, and should attend the formal presentation.

## F. SUMMARY

A management audit is a highly desirable method to review the plans for, or the operations of, a computer application. The audit is performed by an independent function, typically not part of the DP operation nor part of the manager's line of command. The management audit places attention on verifying that processing rules are good management practice and that processing actually follows these rules. A management audit may also be used to check cost-effectiveness of the application.

# 7

# Privacy, security, and backup

## A. INTRODUCTION

A management problem that is important enough to be automated should operate as planned. Human errors, as well as deliberate misuse or abuse of the application or the hardware, frustrate the entire automation effort. Data may be disclosed, modified, or destroyed; equipment may be damaged or destroyed. These risks may threaten any application.

Problems occur more often with especially complex applications that need timeliness, reliability, security, or that run in an environment in which other applications are especially sensitive. Although the loss caused by an application failure may be significant, the costs of prevention cannot be ignored.

This chapter describes privacy, security, and backup from the viewpoint of the manager developing a substantial computer application. The information will be of general interest to the manager working with a non-critical or a small application.

## B. THE PRIVACY ISSUE

### 1. Two Approaches to Privacy

The term "Privacy" is used to indicate that data is kept confidential. The issue of privacy deals with data originating from two different sources: individuals and businesses. The first approach is to view privacy as protecting information on individuals from misuse and disclosure. This protection is especially important in computer applications that identify individuals by name and social security number, and also contain credit information, police records, tax data, medical history, or personal information. An application that contains such information must meet the applicable requirements mandated by federal and state laws for protection from abuse, careless handling, and accidents.

The second approach is to view privacy as protecting company data from misuse by unauthorized personnel within the company, as well as from the general public. Requirements for protecting company data may be stated in written company policy, or may be invoked as part of general management practices. Company financial records, lists of customers, marketing projections, and such are typical of company data that should be kept private.

### 2. Operational Responsibility for Privacy

Responsibility for privacy must be split between the user-manager and the DP center. Equipment on which the application is to be run will be protected from physical access and damage. Protective procedures established by the data center include fire-resistant site construction and locked or guarded doors.

The data center normally establishes manual handling procedures to protect working documents, as well as materials prepared for users. Such procedures include shredding discarded materials (punched cards, listings and such) to prevent inadvertant disclosure, and delivering listings and other materials prepared for users only to authorized personnel. The names of authorized personnel are specified in an authorization memo sent to the computer center. When picking up material, the recipient must present suitable identification, such as a company identification card, or be personally known to the data center employees.

The data center also establishes some degree of protection for user computer application programs and data by its standard operating procedures. Systems software may require would-be users of a terminal to identify themselves with special codes. The user-manager may establish additional codes that limit an authorized terminal user to view data, but not to change data or to modify programs. No users may make changes in the data center's operating systems.

Equipment under the user-manager's control and computer system access through this equipment is the manager's responsibility. Printouts, origianl data entry sheets, program documentation, and identification codes used for the application and maintained in the manager's organization must be protected by that organization. When the material is no longer needed it must be disposed of by burning, shredding or a similar method so that the security of the data is protected.

## C. RISKS AND RISK MANAGEMENT

Every application has potential risks of failure arising from different causes. Risk is the uncertainty of occurrence of a threat that results in a failure. Risks occur in the data, as well as in the processing, as illustrated in Figure 7-1. A broad

FIGURE 7-1 Risks Classified by Source

DATA

- Compromise--Disclosure to Unauthorized Persons
- Error --Input Data Errors
- Loss --Data Garbled, Destroyed

PROCESSING ERRORS, DELAYS AND FAILURE

- In Application Program
- In Computer Manufacturer's Software
- In Computer Equipment
- In Related Manual Processing

viewpoint of risks and risk management that affects an application involves three areas: Risk Analysis, Risk Evaluation, and Risk Management.

## 1. Risk Analysis

There are various methods for appraising the risk of failure. In every instance, the intention is to predict the cost of potential losses, which will provide a basis for planning cost-effective disaster recovery. A formal risk analysis has a higher degree of validity than a purely subjective analysis. However, formal risk analysis methods are misused when they are overly elaborate and of questionable validity. The manager should recognize that all methods are largely subjective and have varying degrees of accuracy. The better methodologies use arbitrary scales, estimate loss potential by classifying threats into similar groups, and use mathematical logic to improve the validity of their findings.

Failure of an application can result from failure of equipment, services, or software that is under the control of either the data processing center or the application manager. This discussion focuses on the risks under the control of the application manager. These failures may be classified into three categories: risks related to data, risks related to the application program design, and risks related to the equipment and the environment.

Data errors may take place while the data is in raw form, as well as any place in the preparation or processing cycle. Raw data is typically reviewed and edited to detect and correct errors before it is processed into machine-usable form. This review and edit process depends upon the effectiveness of manual handling procedures and the skills of the personnel involved. Each technique for transforming raw data into machinable form has its own advantages and limitations. The process of reading and extracting data from hand-written data sheets or printed documents is subject to transcription error. The ease of transcription and the number of errors reflect the legibility and organization of the source information, as well as the training given to personnel making data entries. Review and editing of machinable data is important because subsequent processing and storage is costly and correcting errors forces delays.

The application program design may have unrealistic assumptions about quantity, timeliness, and validity of data. A time-critical report should not depend on availability of all data prior to its production. Input data should always be edited for accuracy to prevent processing errors.

Risks exist because of equipment and environment. If finished data listings are to be sent through regular mail channels, delays must be anticipated in the post office and in the company mail room. Terminals located on factory floors or loading docks may be put out of operation by spilled coffee or by accidental mechanical damage.

## 2. Management Evaluation

Which threats against the application are tolerable and which require protective measures? The preferred approach for a manager is to perform a quick and inexpensive subjective evaluation, to determine whether formal risk analysis is justifiable. If justifiable, perform further evaluation, using more precise quantitative methods. Attempt to answer such questions as: What is the value of the application to the company? What situations threaten success--that is, compromise privacy or security or interfere with timely performance of the application? Has the company encountered problems in similar applications: was a user terminal halted because flooding closed a building entrance or shorted power lines, did lightning or a power surge burn out equipment, have other applications been delayed because of computer center problems?

After defining known security threats, estimate the probability of occurrence. Historic information may be helpful in making these estimates. Each threat may have a different level of potential damage; each level must be estimated to determine just what risks can be avoided by employing protective methods.

## 3. Risk Control

Compare loss prediction to the protection techniques to determine what kinds of protection are effective. You may chose to install protection to avoid a risk, to transfer the risk to others through an insurance arrangement, or to assume the risk. Determine what combination of protective techniques and what degree of their use is most cost-effective for this application. Find out who has control over the various protective measures to be installed.

In some instances, a computer application is not warranted since the risks are so large; that is, if sensitive company data is involved, it may not be suitable to install the application on a computer system that has been, and will continue to be, open to casual users. In such circumstances, a mini-or microcomputer system might be purchased and physically located at the user site solely for the sensitive application. This alternative might be considerably cheaper than running the application on a large central system which requires extensive security upgrading. Another alternative would be to determine the costs for guaranteed computer operating time at another computer center. Such costs might also be less than the costs of protecting the application at the existing data center. Risks may be reduced by using a combination of protective techniques.

## D. PROTECTION CONCEPTS

Protection may be classified in various ways:

1. enhancing reliability or availability,
2. applying physical or technical improvements, or
3. affecting facilities, equipment, people, data, or programs.

Since protection is available in many forms, the concepts of protection tend to be vague in many discussions, and only become clear after discussing specific technical or physical improvements to satisfy a specific application.

Protection for a computer application depends in part on the protection already provided by the supporting computer center. The protection specific to an application includes:

1. protection of the user site against physical damage,
2. protection of user-controlled equipment,
3. protection of data used in the application, and
4. protection of the applications software (programs).

## 1. User Site Protection

Methods that protect a user's site from physical damage are similar to methods used to protect any major computer center, differing only in the degree of protection provided and the size of the site. Three protective techniques are commonly used: concealing the facility, protecting the physical facility perimeter, and protecting the site environment.

Frequently, a small user site facility is hidden from potential intruders by eliminating identifying signs and room numbers, and by locating the site in an out-of-the-way corridor of a building or inside a much larger restricted area. This technique is inexpensive and may be practical, especially when the user facility is located within a large building or building complex. A user application that deals with valuable assets, such as securities, diamonds, furs, or foreign exchange may require very little space to house the necessary terminals. Because of the importance of such applications, they often have the additional protection of heavy fireproof walls and, perhaps, a guarded or card-controlled entrance door. Since regular continued use of terminals is so important to many user applications, the user site may also have special fire protection, such as hand extinguishers, a sprinkler system, a nontoxic gas fire-suppression system, plus smoke and heat detectors in floors and ceilings. Separate air conditioning and filtered or conditioned electrical power for the terminals, plus batteries and emergency lighting, may also be provided.

Initiate an audit of the physical environment by identifying the application and the circumstances surrounding it. Figure 7-2, Physical Protection Audit Overview, outlines the factors to include.

## 2. User-Controlled Equipment Protection

Equipment within the user site may be protected from physical damage by heavy duty construction, enclosure in protective covers, and protection of its power, cooling, and communications. Computer equipment built for military use is often built with extra heavy frames and chassis, as well as shock resistant internal connections. Typical commercial terminals and printers to be used on a loading dock may be protected from wind and rain by canopies and covers or by housing them in their own

FIGURE 7-2 Physical Protection Audit Overview

1. Application Name ______________________________

______________________________

2. Application Manager (Name and Phone) ______________

______________________________

3. Number of different class of terminal devices ________

______________________________

4. Number terminals/devices assigned to each class ______

______________________________

5. Auditor(s) ______________________________

6. Terminal/device audited ______________________________

7. Describe application privacy & security requirements

______________________________

______________________________

______________________________

______________________________

______________________________

______________________________

specially-built room. If a device must be used in a dusty factory area, filters may be needed to protect fan motors and components from abrasion and short circuits. Electrical power is often obtained by plugging a device into the nearest wall socket. Many areas of the country have had problems with electrical power, blackouts, brownouts, transients, or voltage surges. Electrical problems can halt or cause erratic operation of computer terminals and equipment. In some cases, the equipment has been physically damaged or destroyed. Since equipments have varying sensitivity to power aberrations, some protection may be needed and can be obtained through regulation and protection devices, such as surge suppressors, isolated power supplies, motor generator sets, and uninterruptable power supplies. Proper equipment cooling is a necessity. The need differs between equipment, location, and conditions of use. Terminals located in office areas may not have adequate cooling, if the office air conditioning system is marginal, or if the office was not designed for terminals. Supplementary air conditioning, in the form of window units, or rebuilding of a central air conditioning system may be necessary.

Typical communications between terminals, printers, and a computer system involve hard copper wires, fiber optics, or a variety of coaxial and broadband cables. Often, the terminal may have to be connected to the computer center over telephone company facilities. Protection is needed for the data transmission process, since data may be intercepted and read or altered, depending upon the naure of this connection.

Application security requires that an appropriate level of physical protection be provided for user equipment. When multiple terminals can be used, the failure of any single unit does not stop the application, so that special protection of any single terminal is not necessary. If the terminals are placed in widely separated locations, failure of one terminal will effectively stop the users at that location from entering data or receiving reports for that application. If the application information must be kept confidential, all the communications connections must be protected from access.

Key locks are often used to prevent unauthorized parties from tampering with equipment settings. Equipment that has a paper or card feeder, or includes a removable floppy disk, tape cassette, or tape reel can be put out of commission by mishandling or by use of warped or damaged disks or cassettes.

The principal items to be reviewed for a user site are shown in Figure 7-3. The items include the size of the site, amount of concealment, use of perimeter walls, protection of entries and environment. A large user site may require a more extensive checklist. Review individual terminal protection with a checklist in the format shown in Figure 7-4. This checklist might be modified for more elaborate terminals located in a hazardous environment.

FIGURE 7-3 User Site Protection Checklist

Physical Site Identification ______________________________

______________________________

| | | Rating 3 | 2 | 1 |
|---|---|---|---|---|
| 1. | Size | Adequate | Poor | Crowded |
| 2. | Concealment | Excellent | Good | Poor |
| 3. | Perimeter Walls | Entry-proof | Resistant | Fragile |
| 4. | No. of Entrances | 1-2 | 3-4 | 5 plus |
| 5. | Entrance Protection | Card, key handprint, etc. | Some Restriction | Open access |
| 6. | Fire & Smoke Detectors | Automatic floor & ceiling | Some | None |
| 7. | Fire Protection | Sprinkler or halon system | Hand extinguishers | None |
| 8. | Power/AC Cutoffs | Emergency cutoffs at entry | Some cutoffs | None |

FIGURE 7-4 User Equipment Protection Checklist

Equipment: ______________________________

| | | Rating 3 | 2 | 1 |
|---|---|---|---|---|
| 1. | Smoke, Dust, Fume & Fire Protection | Excellent | Some | None |
| 2. | Physical Shock Protection | Excellent | Some | None |
| 3. | Power Protection | Power protect Equip in place per consultant's specification | Some | None |
| 4. | Communications Line | Protected to engineering specification | Some | None |
| 5. | Air Conditioning | Fully Adequate | Adequate | None |

## 3. Application Data Protection

Data used in an application must be properly collected, edited, processed, and stored. All data should be accurately collected and meet the expected collection time schedule: sales data is to be collected by 6:00 P.M., data must be received from all sales representatives, data must be checked before and after transmission to insure that it is complete and correct. If a terminal has failed, the application software should at the minimum record the failure. Although a terminal failure does not breech security, it can allow data to remain uncorrected, as well as prevent normal updating, so that summary reports may not be corrected.

Complete and correct data entry is often aided by use of self-checking forms. If data entry is performed directly on an intelligent terminal, a format may be presented on the face of the CRT to assist in proper data entry in each field, such as must be numeric, must have six characters, must be completed. If the entry is made through the terminal to a computer, the computer may be programmed to respond, indicating that the data entry was correct or that it must be reentered. Figure 7-5 is a checklist that reviews the completeness and accuracy of the data used in an application.

FIGURE 7-5 User Application Data Checklist

Application: ______________________________

______________________________

| | | Rating 3 | 2 | 1 |
|---|---|---|---|---|
| 1. | Data Entry Instructions | Clear & Complete | Good | Poor |
| 2. | Timeliness of Data Entry | Always on time | Rarely late | Late |
| 3. | Entries Are Complete | Always | Almost always | Sometimes incorrect |
| 4. | Volume of Entries | Within plans | Rarely outside plans | Often outside plans |
| 5. | Frequency of Data Entry | Within plans | Rarely outside plans | Often outside plans |
| 6. | No of Data Sources | Within plans | Rarely exceeds | Often exceeds |

## 4. Application Software Protection

A computer application may require a number of computer programs of varying complexity. The more critical and complex the application, the more important it is to be assured that the computer programs perform as intended. Programs should process valid data, reject or tag and reject erroneous data, produce results as predicted, and store data as planned. Figure 7-6, Applications Software Checklist 1, is a checklist for reviewing the general adequacy of program design to determine that the program is itself complete. Figure 7-7 Applications Software Checklist 2, is a checklist dealing with the operation of the computer program. It focuses on control of access, proper operation, control of changes in the program, and use of standard test data.

### 5. Privacy and Security Checklists

Major lapses in privacy and security tend to be violations of good general management policy. An important aspect of every audit is to insure that good management policies are planned and followed. Audit checklists serve to insure that the important questions are not overlooked. Coordinate the answers resulting from a checklist to arrive at an overall judgment. To this end, different answers to a question are given different numeric values. These values are summed up to produce a total for the checklist; this total is a measure of how well security and privacy is maintained. The numeric scale chosen for a checklist reflects the judgment of the people who construct the checklist, as does the selection of the questions. Checklists shown in Figures 7-3 through 7-7 use a scale of 1, 2, 3, and award the highest score for the best results. Other scales could be used.

## E. BACKUP

A secure, reliable application is available when needed and operates as planned. Since computer equipment and software failures cannot be completely eliminated, the only way to insure that an application will be available is to provide backup. The amount and extent of backup required depends upon the nature of the application. The amount provided depends upon the cost involved.

Backup for computer applications may be classified as manual or automated, partial or total, or as available immediately or with delay, as shown in Figure 7-8.

FIGURE 7-6 Applications Software Checklist 1

Application: ______________________________

______________________________

Program: ______________________________

______________________________

| | | Rating 3 | 2 | 1 |
|---|---|---|---|---|
| 1. | Data Inputs Are Specified | Completely | Almost Completely | Some Exceptions |
| 2. | Program Inputs Are Specified | Completely | Almost Completely | Some Exceptions |
| 3. | Exceptions Identified | Always | Almost Always | Some Exceptions |
| 4. | Exceptions Processing Specified | Always | Minor Exception | More Than Minor Exceptions |
| 5. | Exceptions are Processed Correctly | Always | Minor Exception | Exceptions |
| 6. | Acceptable Data Is Processed Correctly | Always | Minor Exception | Exceptions |

FIGURE 7-7 Applications Software Checklist 2

Application: ____________________

____________________

Program: ____________________

| | | Rating 3 | 2 | 1 |
|---|---|---|---|---|
| 1. | Program Access Restricted | Yes | Rare exceptions | Exceptions |
| 2. | Program Access Restricted to Few People | 2 or less | 3-5 | Over 5 |
| 3. | Change Access Restricted | 2 or less | 3-5 | Over 5 |
| 4. | Program Changes Tested & Signed Before Accepted | Yes | Almost always | Exceptions |
| 5. | Program Changes Recorded | Yes | Almost always | Exceptions |
| 6. | Program Change Records Reviewed by Management | Yes | Almost always | Exceptions |
| 7. | Standard Test Data Used | Yes | Almost always | Exceptions |
| 8. | Standard Test Data Used to Verify Program Changes | Yes | Rare Exceptions | Exceptions |

FIGURE 7-8 Backup Alternatives

MANUAL SYSTEM

- Partial Backup
- Full Backup

SIMPLIFIED OR COMPLETE AUTOMATED BACKUP

- At a service bureau or time-share vendor
- At the company computer center
- On a small computer at the user location
- On a word processor at the user location

DELAYED AUTOMATED BACKUP

- The empty shell
  - User supplies equipment, supplies, people
  - Some support
  - The shared computer center
  - Voluntary sharing
    - with priorities
    - with some available capacity
  - Sharing contracts
    - with priorities
    - with some available capacity
- The spare computer center
  - Full duplicate center
  - Unused versus used on an as-available basis

If a computer failure is not a major physical disaster, such as a fire, an area-wide power outage, or earthquake, a minimum level of protection at the equipment site may provide adequate backup. However, backup is only assured if the application may be freely operated at a different site, using a full duplicate set of equipment with copies of the software and up-to-date files, along with personnel who know how to run the equipment and the application. If the application requires a considerable amount of computer running time, the backup computer system must have the time available, or the manager may have a conflict with another user or have to pay to obtain a priority.

Each type of backup arrangement has different costs and provides a different set of benefits. Backup for security, privacy, and reliability must be suitable to the application. The complex application may need and warrant costly backup features as shown in Figure 7-9.

FIGURE 7-9 Major Backup Requirements

* Duplicate Computer System/User Terminals (or arrange to obtain on an expedited basis)
* Data Communications Service
* Copies of Data Files
* Copy of Application Documentation
* Identical Systems Software (including same revision levels)
* Stock of Specialized Forms
* Delivery Arrangements for Input and Output Documents and Reports
* Arrangements for Payment/Reimbursement for Equipment and Services Costs
* Trained Operations Personnel
* Computer Operations Documentation, including Instructions, Manuals, and Test Data
* Cutover Procedures for Data Processing Personnel
* Cutover Procedures for Users

Review backup for costs and capabilities implied in the original design specifications. Evaluate the costs of appropriate backup in terms of the need for reliable and secure processing. Typical questions to ask about backup for terminals are shown in Figure 7-10, Terminal Equipment Backup Checklist.

FIGURE 7-10 Terminal Equipment Backup Checklist

| | | Rating 3 | Rating 2 | Rating 1 |
|---|---|---|---|---|
| 1. | Are backup needs stated in application documentation? | Yes | Partially | No |
| 2. | Are backup needs implied by system design? | Yes | Partially | No |
| 3. | Has backup been tested? | Yes | Partially | No |
| 4. | Has backup been tested in full operation? | Yes | Partially | No |
| 5. | Are backup plans fully documented? | Yes | Partially | No |
| 6. | When were backup plans formally updated? | Within 1 Year | Over 1 Year Less than 2 | Over 2 Years |
| 7. | Are all parties concerned with activating the backup named with contact phone numbers in the backup plan? | Yes | Partially | No |
| 8. | Has the backup plan been reviewed for cost-effectiveness? | Yes | Partially | No |

If the application is operated at a service bureau, or if there is a reasonable possibility of moving the application to a different data processing center, perform some evaluation of the current and the alternate center. A basic checklist is shown in Figure 7-11, Security Checklist for the Data Center.

FIGURE 7-11 Security Checklist for the Data Center

| | | Rating 3 Yes | 2 Partially | 1 No |
|---|---|---|---|---|
| 1. | Does the center have a satisfactory access control program? | | | |
| 2. | Does the center have a satisfactory fire prevention, detection and control system? | | | |
| 3. | Does the computer center have emergency power cutoffs, exits, floor drains, air conditioning cutoffs? | | | |
| 4. | Does the center train its people in using protective plans and methods? | | | |
| 5. | Does the center monitor and control movement of center employees, vendors, telephone, and maintenance people? | | | |
| 6. | Does the center monitor and act quickly to eliminate equipment failure? | | | |
| 7. | Is disposal of old or duplicate paper listings, tapes, etc. secure? | | | |
| 8. | Does the center maintain backup files for user data and programs? | | | |
| 9. | Does the center store data files in a restricted and physically protected area? | | | |
| 10. | Does the center have an effective program to control software access? | | | |
| 11. | Does the center maintain a master security program and test it regularly? | | | |
| 12. | Does the center have a backup plan and test it regularly? | | | |

## F. COSTS OF BACKUP

A brief quantitative analysis by a concerned manager could be useful, inexpensive, and available quickly. To perform such a brief analysis, take the sum of the costs of the major losses times their probability and compare this sum to the estimated costs of backup from an outside vendor. A preliminary analysis of this type directs attention to the size of the losses, which indicates the potential benefits that a specific protective measure provides. This type of study is often termed a "quick and dirty" analysis, suggesting that the analysis is poor. The important point is that such an analysis is inexpensive and is generally cost-effective. Such an analysis is more accurately identified as a preliminary gross study. A typical format to use is shown in Figure 7-12, Preliminary Analysis for Application Backup.

FIGURE 7-12 Preliminary Analysis for Application Backup

| Risk | $ Cost | Estimated Probability | Annual Loss |
|---|---|---|---|
| Local Fire | $ 5,000 | 1 in 5 years | $ 1,000 |
| Major Fire | $100,00 | 1 in 100 years | $ 1,000 |
| Earthquake | $ 20,000 | 1 in 100 years | $ 200 |
| Riot | $ 10,000 | 1 in 10 years | $ 1,000 |
| Minor Power Failure | $ 5,000 | 4 times year | $ 20,000 |
| Major Power Failure | $100,000 | 1 time year | $100,000 |
| Employee Error | $ 20,000 | 2 times year | $ 40,000 |
| Deliberate Employee Abuse/Mishandling | $250,000 | 2 times year | $ 40,000 |
| User Mishandling | $ 50,000 | | |
| ⋮ | ⋮ | ⋮ | ⋮ |

Data entered in Figure 7-12 should reflect the manager's appraisal of risk, cost, and probability. If values assumed in this example are true for the specific application, the manager should ask the data processing center about the cost of power protection and should also consider the costs that might be incurred to maintain backup data, software, and so on at another data center.

A more precise analysis and review of privacy, security, and backup costs and benefits may be performed in the same logical fashion as the earlier analysis and review. However, this later analysis and review can be restricted in scope by considering only the additional costs incurred and comparing them to the losses occurring when the application fails. This reduced form of analysis tends to be performed infrequently, since it:

a. depends upon the availability of a previously performed and documented cost/benefit analysis,
b. must apply some estimates of the frequency and duration of failures to determine failure costs, and
c. requires expertise in economic and accounting analysis, as well as knowledge of computer technology and management.

The difficulty of performing this analysis and the uncertainty of failures may introduce a degree of skepticism as to the reliability of the results. Detailed analysis and review is best justified when large protection costs are likely or the application is critical.

## G. SUMMARY

Privacy, security, and backup reflect the needs of the application and its design. It is important in planning to recognize the legal and general business requirements. It is also important to recognize that there are many different cost tradeoffs possible between risks and protective measures. A quick preliminary analysis helps the manager determine what is required for a specific application and guides further analysis. Later detail analysis of costs and benefits refines original estimates and is desirable when risks are significant and protection costs are high.

# 8

# Trends in automation

## A. INTRODUCTION

The ability to develop a computer application is increasingly important to every successful manager. Although the logic of the development process may be clear, the tools and techniques used in the process are continually changing. A brief review of significant computer development trends is important in selecting the best tools and techniques for a specific application. In a broad sense, these trends may be categorized as a series of changes in computer equipment, human resources, communications, and computer applications. Understanding these changes will give you an opportunity to plan new and improved applications. Existing applications may be extended into locations previously not considered, or expanded to serve more complex needs. This chapter describes these changes and concludes with an appraisal of future applications.

## B. TECHNICAL TRENDS IN COMPUTER EQUIPMENT

Computer equipment has benefited by the development of increasingly dense and reliable computer chips. Despite their small physical size, the chips can and do contain increasingly powerful circuits for performing complex functions. As a result, computer equipment has become physically smaller and more powerful. This development of sophisticated circuitry has been accompanied by continuous improvements in manufacturing processes, so that increasingly large amounts of storage and faster storage access can be offered at decreasing prices.

Technical trends in hardware are seen in such areas as improved terminals, including graphic and color devices, home and personal computers, optical character readers, adaption of electric typewriters as low cost computer printers, and combining word processing and data processing on the same terminal. Many users see this hardware development because of its effects on computer terminals:

a. Portable terminals are readily available in the ten-to-twenty-pound range and can be built into an attache case.
b. Terminals used in office and factory situations are more sophisticated, and commonly feature large readable displays and easy-to-use keyboards.
c. Terminals are available with large amounts of internal data storage, so that they may automatically perform some data-editing at the time the user enters information.
d. Terminals are available to provide output to users in graphic form. Graphic terminals translate columns of numbers directly into bar charts, pie charts, and trend lines, and often include color. Terminal capabilities range from simple line drawings in black and white to fully colored illustrations with complex graphics.
e. Printers and plotters are available to translate graphic terminal images into paper copies, and in some instances, add color or produce a 35 mm slide or a transparency. Decreasing hardware prices and improved software make terminals increasingly cost-effective.

Optical character recognition equipment has been in existence for many years. The high costs involved and their operational limitations restricted their use to large-volume, specialized applications, such as post office letter sorting, gasoline charge slip processing, and similar. Prices have dropped, and product quality and capability have increased, so that OCR equipment has become cost-competitive for applications involving typed materials. Further cost reduction and capability improvement are expected which will make OCR an effective technique for bulk text-editing, whenever a sufficiently large quantity of word processing units (5-15) are located together. The difficulty of applying OCR to improve computer applications will, in many instances, reflect a lack of professionals skilled in applying such equipment, rather than limitations in the equipment itself.

Adapting electric typewriters as letter-quality low-cost terminals has an impact on many organizations. Since hundreds of thousands of typewriters are already in place, user costs to modify each unit are low, compared to purchasing a separate computer-printing device. This low cost may allow many organizations that cannot justify large computer expenditures to automate small offices.

Electronic typewriters have had continual price reduction since their introduction. If this downward price trend continues, they will supplant standard electric typewriters. Electronic typewriter purchasers are likely to favor those machines which have easy-to-add features, such as communications to allow the typewriter to be used as a computer terminal. Many electronic typewriters are designed to have communication added with a plug-in module.

Another effect of increasing computer power and reducing costs has been to increase computer equipment sales and attract new manufacturers. Competition among these computer manufacturers has resulted in many types of equipment being marketed, including reliable low-cost small computer systems available for personal and business computing purposes.

Word processing to produce documents and data processing to manipulate data have generally required the use of separate devices. Frequently, keyboards, printing mechanisms, and other features of these devices have been completely different. A number of manufacturers now offer a single terminal device to perform both services. Locations that could not economically justify two separate terminals may be able to justify the lower cost of a single combined terminal. Not all word processing and data processing uses are compatible; when on-line receipt of data processing information is expected, the terminal device cannot be used for editing documents. Typists and programmers have different performance needs that may conflict. A single terminal may be ineffective in this situation. If separate devices are used, they can be optimized for specific jobs; the better printing quality needed for letter writing is more expensive than the printing quality needed for DP use.

Future use of combined word processing/data processing (WP/DP) will increase, especially where low-usage locations have minimal interference between word processing and data processing needs. However, increasing professional and clerical salaries may justify separate devices, even in low-usage locations to maximize the improvements in personnel productivity. Large organizations are likely to use separate work processing and data processing, as well as combined WP/DP devices.

## C. HUMAN RESOURCES

Recent studies indicate several demographic trends affecting the future United States workforce in the years 1992 and 2000. One predicted trend relates birth rates to occupational choices, and projects both a relative and absolute shortage of clerical and secretarial personnel. The second trend relates occupational choices to personnel availability, and projects a further decrease in the supply of clerical and secretarial personnel, as women increasingly choose professional careers. An equally important development which should be considered is the widespread availability of computer training in business schools and colleges. This will mean that more professional and technical personnel will have experience in using computer equipment.

Many organizations find that an increasing proportion of their payroll is going to support technical and professional persons, whose salaries are in the range of $2,000--$5,000 a month. Cost-effective applications that automate and replace substantial amounts of clerical processing time may become less important than applications that save technical and professional time. An illustration of automation savings with word processing (see Figure 8-1) is suggestive of the future direction of automation.

FIGURE 8-1 Automated Word Processing

## 1. Automating a Clerical Application

A. GIVEN:

| | | |
|---|---|---|
| 1. | WP Machine (Purchase) | $15,000 |
| 2. | 5-year Amortization | $ 3,000 |
| 3. | Annual Clerical Employee Cost | $15,000 |

B. CLERICAL SUPPORT VIA WP:

| | | |
|---|---|---|
| 1. | 50% employee's time on WP | $ 7,500 |
| 2. | 100% productivity improvement-benefit | $ 7,500 |

C. COST VS. BENEFIT COMPARISON:*

| | | |
|---|---|---|
| 1. | Annual Benefit/Annual Cost | 2 1/2 to 1 |
| 2. | Equipment Payback (Accounting) | 2 years |

*NOTE: Assume that supply savings equal annual maintenance cost.

## 2. Automating a Technical/Professional Application

A. GIVEN:

| | | |
|---|---|---|
| 1. | WP Machine (Purchase) | $15,000 |
| 2. | 5-year Amortization | $ 3,000 |
| 3. | Annual Professional Employee Cost | $24-60,000 |

B. PROFESSIONAL SUPPORT VIA WP:

| | | |
|---|---|---|
| 1. | Review Typed Material 3 hours daily<br>Save 2 hours by reading only changes | |
| 2. | 25% employee saving | $6,000-15,000 |

C. COST VS. BENEFIT COMPARISON:

| | | |
|---|---|---|
| 1. | Annual Benefit/Annual Cost | 2 to 1; 5 to 1 |
| 2. | Equipment Payback | 1 to 2 1/2 years |

CONCLUSION: Automation for professionals may be a significant cost-saving opportunity.

## D. DEVELOPMENTS IN COMMUNICATIONS

Many data processing applications require terminals and computers to be installed outside of the company data processing center. Part of this distribution of processing has also involved transmitting information between locations. Communications developments include:

a. Special Communications Services,
b. Local Distribution Networks,
c. The Wired City,
d. The Digital Switch, and
e. Fiber Optics.

Escalating tariff rates have made communications costs a large percentage of the total cost of operating an aplicaton, and considerable effort is being spent to minimize these communications costs. Low volume, low speed usage may be satisfied by using dial-up telephone service from the local telephone company. A special type of communications service (packet switching) is increasingly effective when medium speed (1,200-4,800 bps) communications must be supported, and when widespread usage is involved, but when volumes are not large enough to warrant private lines. Several private carriers offer this service. If concentrated high volumes and high speeds are involved, private leased lines become more cost-effective.

The local telephone company is being challenged by private telephone companies, which may provide competitive service to key cities only, service for computer type data only, or service for another type of general communications. Tariff rates differ between the conventional telephone companies and these other specialized carriers, and the differences do not remain constant. An application using a widespread assortment of telephone lines should be reviewed frequently to assure the lowest cost tariff charges.

The concentration of terminals around a typical local computer center, and the costs of local communications lines, has focused attention on a variety of less costly local communications systems to use within buildings, and to link offices in nearby buildings. These systems include coaxial and broadband cable, radio frequency (RF) distribution systems, as well as sophisticated systems utilizing conventional copper wires.

One popular concept of low-cost local networks has been described in terms of a "wired city." The implication is that every home and office in a metropolitan area will be connected inexpensively by a network of wires or cables. The application of this technique for business or industrial use may be ineffective, especially in view of the higher speeds and concentrated usage in many business applications. The technique may be appropriate for applications in which a large percentage of the general population is involved.

A possible alternative communications network for some local business applications is to use an inhouse digital telephone switch (an intelligent PBX) to connect terminals at local office locations to a local computer center. This requires that all terminals and the computer site are served by the same telephone switch, that is, they are in the same private company switchboard. Digital switches are commonly limited to passing asynchronous data traffic, and must have additional circuitry to handle synchronous traffic. In addition, such telephone switches must have appropriate connections available for every office. The adoption of such an innovative communications technique is best approached by recognizing technical limitations now existing, examining the cost advantages expected over the next few years, and evaluating anticipated communications loads.

Fiber optics communications lines may allow future applications to be feasible, because these lines can carry computer data through unusual environments. Frequently, a planned application may be cheaper to implement and cost-effective if terminals communicate with the computer directly, rather than through modems and other special communications equipment. A fiber optics line connecting to a terminal may be run directly through a steam tunnel, through elevator shafts, around heavy power equipment, through power conduits, around radio transmitters, and next to welding equipment, since it is nonconducting and unaffected by magnetism. Since fibers are a form of glass, and carry light beams, fiber optic lines can be safely run through water and other liquids.

## E. COMPUTER APPLICATION DEVELOPMENTS

Software developments are not as obvious as hardware innovations, but are equally important. New software is typically built upon old software and corrects defects, as well as adding new capabilities. Computer applications packages are rapidly increasing in quantity and quality. The potential costs and time savings by use of these packages will be important. Managers and business people are likely to spend more time evaluating application packages and their costs, and seeking cost trade-offs in relation to the required features of a proposed application program. Emphasis on costs may shift attitudes toward use of a package, even if the package does not do everything desired. Licensing agreements will become more important, since multiple site usage of the same package is likely in distributed applications.

Special applications of computers are made possible by increasingly sophisticated instructions (software programs). Trends appear in such areas as prototyping applications on a micro, protocol translation, bar coding, use of data base systems, and English language software.

Low cost personal and business computers may find a special use for proposed applications. When the application is complex, it may be possible to have a simple version programmed quickly and at a nominal cost. The results of this prototyping effort may be to identify potential problems in the proposed application at an early stage, when other approaches can be readily considered, such as, when proposed terminals would operate too slowly to satisfy customers, or when communications traffic will be so large as to require more service and higher costs. At the same time, other alternative solutions may be suggested. If certain types of equipment are preferred, the company computer center and computer experts should be notified to fully explain this possibility in their long-range planning.

Computer and word processing equipment from the same manufacturer may not be compatible. If a user expects to operate a printer supplied by one manufacturer with a computer terminal from another, problems of compatability often arise. Incompatibility between one manufacturer's central processing unit (CPU) and another manufacturer's terminals is common, as is incompatibility between word procesing and computer equipment, and between different word processing units. These incompatibilities have made it very expensive for one user to share data or information directly with another user.

A class of devices and services have developed to provide compatibility, including:

a. protocol translation devices for CRT's (and terminals),
b. protocol translation devices for communicating between unlike word processing terminals,
c. devices to transfer data from one style floppy disk to another, and
d. devices to accept information via communications lines (or from disks) as input to phototypesetting equipment. Word processing and data processing manufacturers may offer some types of protocol translation on their equipment.

Translation between CRT's and low speed terminals to computer systems allows low cost ASCII terminals to be used with existing computer systems. This type of protocol translator capability makes it cost-effective to provide inexpensive terminals at low-usage locations without changing the application.

Translation between word processing terminals allows documents to be edited and revised in a different machine, without the time delay and cost of rekeying the material. When floppy disk translation equipment is available, it likewise eliminates rekeying. There are some devices and techniques that allow data to be entered directly into phototypesetting equipment. Again, this process eliminates the time and cost of rekeying data.

None of the translation techniques are completely trouble free. However, since these techniques can be important cost savers, they are being used more frequently. Hardware and software costs involved are decreasing. As these costs decrease, and services become more widely available, the manager may be able to effectively extend an application onto existing equipment. This development will lend itself to wider use of standard company applications.

Bar coding techniques and bar code labels are familiar to many as a result of their use on grocery and household items. The costs of using the bar code technique are concentrated in the associated data processing equipment. The same techniques are used in inventory applications characterized by large quantities and moderate item values, such as library book circulation. Bar coding is also cost-effective when the labor costs for taking inventory are significant, as in inventory of office equipment and furniture.

Data base management systems (DBMS) manage the information stored by users. The more powerful the tool, the more skill required to use it properly. Improvements in DBMS continue to reduce the cost of subsequent computer processing for an application, and improve the speed and ease of obtaining results. The manager will be concerned about this software if:

a. the manager has many applications,
b. the manager expects to have many applications in the same functional area,
c. the manager's application must use or supply information to other applications that utilize a DBMS, or
d. company policy dictates use of a DBMS.

English language software is continuing to be developed. Data processing people expect to use COBOL, FORTRAN, PL1 and similar languages to direct the computer. In recent years, however, computer vendors have expended considerable effort in making their equipment easier to use, especially for people without formal programming training. The spread of the BASIC computer language and various adaptations illustrates this trend. Additional techniques have been developed by many manufacturers to lead their terminal users through the correct operating steps in completing a form, entering an order entry, and such. In some computer and word processing terminals, lists of instructions appear on the screen at the touch of a "help" button.

## F. CONCLUSIONS

A number of trends affect the success of a proposed computer application, including increases in computer power and price reductions for this equipment. At the same time professional and clerical labor costs are increasing, so that proposed automation becomes a more cost-effective solution. More effective applications result when related trends in improved communications, and use of appropriate packaged software, are incorporated. The most effective solutions result when a manager's plans are in sufficient detail to prevent problems and take advantage of opportunities as they occur.

# Index